41594899

Reengineering Software

How to Reuse
Programming
to Build New,
State-of-the-Art
Software
Second Edition

Roy Rada

Glenlake Publishing Company, Ltd.
Chicago • London • New Delhi

AMACOM
American Management Association
New York • Atlanta • Boston • Chicago • Kansas City
San Francisco • Washington, D.C.
Brussels • Mexico City • Tokyo • Toronto

This publication is designed to provide accurate and authoritative information in regard to the subject matter covered. It is sold with the understanding that the publisher is not engaged in rendering legal, accounting, or other professional service. If legal advice or other expert assistance is required, the services of a competent professional person should be sought.

AMACOM
American Management Association
New York • Atlanta • Boston • Chicago • Kansas City • San Francisco • Washington, D.C.
Brussels • Mexico City • Tokyo • Toronto

Printing number
10 9 8 7 6 5 4 3 2 1

Contents

Preface

At first glance, software reuse appears a natural way to develop software, but in practice this does not happen. The challenges are numerous and require a fresh approach to the entire range of activities involved in the engineering of software. Every time new software is needed developers tend to write from scratch rather than harness components developed through previous projects. Why this is so and how it can be changed will be explored in this book.

This book addresses the state of the art, principles, approaches, support systems, underlying methodologies and real cases in software reuse. Document-oriented versus object-oriented approaches to reuse are discussed and compared and some software reuse support systems, incorporating both approaches, are described. Standards are emphasized, as is the influence of the World Wide Web in the spread of reuse practice. The *theme* throughout is that reuse is fundamental to software engineering but under-appreciated and under-practiced.

First Edition

The first drafts of this book began in 1988 when Section 1, 'Background,' was written for a course on software engineering. Section 2, 'Reuse Processes' and Section 3, 'Practical Examples,' began with the joining of Roy Rada s research group in the European ESPRIT Practitioner Project on software reuse. Three researchers at the University of Liverpool, Weigang Wang, Karl Strickland, and Cornelia Boldyreff, were particularly active in the Practitioner work. Hafedh Mili of the University of Quebec at Montreal is the leader of the SoftClass project that is described in this book and was a regular contributor to the Practitioner project. Many of Mili s ideas and descriptions are included in this book. Important other participants in the Practitioner project who indirectly contributors to this book include Lene Olsen, Jan Witt, Peter Elzer, and Jurgen Heger. In 1992 Stuart MacGlashan and Michelle Usher began work on background material for the book and in 1993 Renata Malinowski and Claude Ghaoui became active contributors. All of the above listed people deserve a very major thanks for their contributions. Stuart MacGlashan particularly invested a large amount of time in developing textual and graphical content and took the book as his special project. He deserves the largest acknowledgement.

The first edition of this book was published in 1995. The author believes in reuse and the book was intended to show how a systematic approach to document reuse can lead to good results. In the end, the concerted efforts of Stuart and then Roy were required to bring cohesiveness to the book. A team of people involved in reuse must communicate extensively to produce one seamless product and this was more easily achieved by one person working for a long time than many people working for a short time. The outline of the original book was based on a published paper that had a balanced outline which is based on organizing, finding, and reorganizing documents and objects (Rada *et al*, 1992). Based on earlier work (Rada and You, 1992), this balanced outline was expected to guide the collaborative production of a cohesive book. In the end, relatively little of the book, only parts of Section 2 actually reflected this balanced outline. Again the expectations for reuse are not always reflected in practice. The jury is still debating about the best ways to achieve reuse. The question is not whether reuse is good but rather how to identify the circumstances in which reuse can be effective. Reuse depends not only on the character of the available information but also on the management of the authoring team. The contributors to this book are committed not only to further exploration of the principles of reuse, but also to the practice of reuse in everyday affairs.

Second Edition

One of the greatest impacts on reuse is the widespread accessibility of document and software archives through the World Wide Web. The spread of the web has also stimulated further development of software and information systems whose components can be reused. In other words, the needs and opportunities for reuse have significantly grown.

Since this book appeared in 1995, several other reuse books have appeared on the market—a good sign of the topic s increasing importance. The other new books fall into a few, general categories: selected conference papers, managing software reuse, special tools or libraries for reuse, and general reuse overviews. For example, new books in the category of selected conference papers include a conference on correctness and reusability (Wieringa and Feenstra, 1995). Such a book is more focused and less cohesive than this book. In the topic of managing reuse were new books by Lim (1995) and Tracz (1995) that were specifically about managing or institutionalizing software reuse. The book in your hand does emphasize the importance of managerial and institutional approaches to software reuse, but covers, in some depth, the more asset specific topics. In the category of special tools are many books, such as a book on reusable Unix software (Krishnamurthy, 1995) and one on reuse metrics (Poulin, 1997). The book in your hand addresses reuse of Unix software components and metrics of reuse but only as part of the book rather than the theme of the book.

Finally comes the category of general-purpose book into which this book falls. Here there seem to be fewer books than in the other three categories but still the reader has options. For instance, the book by Bassett (1997) suits the strong, contemporary interest in frameworks. This particular book is less scholarly in its intentions than the book in your hand. Comparisons could continue in this fashion but suffice it to say that this book attempts to cover the field broadly and concisely. Furthermore, this second edition has been updated to reflect developments of the past two years.

The book is divided into four major sections entitled:

1. Background

2. Enterprise and Standards

3. Organize, Retrieve, and Reorganize

4. Practical Examples

The Background Section looks at the software life cycle and software management. The Enterprise and Standards Section presents first a conceptual framework for reuse that emphasizes enterprise issues and second the important standards are germane to reuse. The Organize, Retrieve, and Reorganize Section examines reuse from the perspective of organizing a library, retrieving items from the library, and reorganizing or tailoring the assets thus retrieved to make a new product. The Practical

Examples Section considers tools, case studies of organizations, and takes a special look at the domain of courseware reuse.

The chapter on software reuse standards is new to the second edition. It is based on the work of the Software Engineering Standards Committee Reuse Group and columns co-authored with James Moore. The software engineering community has decided that object-oriented engineering is not the panacea that it was once claimed to be and is now talking about patterns and frameworks. Patterns and frameworks extend the object-oriented paradigm to deal at a larger level of granularity. This trend towards patterns and frameworks is reflected in various sections of the book.

The courseware chapter has been augmented with new results in the form of web-based libraries of reusable components and standards for courseware reuse. Courseware serves as an example of the kind of developments that one would find across many domains in which increased web access and demand for software has lead to new libraries and high-level tool sets. Furthermore, courseware about reuse could be important in supporting education about reuse itself. A key barrier to improved reuse practice is the lack of adequate education about reuse itself.

The author and publisher of this book want to build on the value of the information superhighway to the reader. Accordingly, the book is available for free in electronic form on the World Wide Web—this distinguishes the book further from the other books on reuse. Also the book is integrated into a virtual classroom and is available in that way on the web. The book and the course can be found by visiting the author s home page on the web. The author is also helping create a Virtual Information Technology College under the sponsorship of the Globewide Network Academy. Part of the intention of the new college is that teachers, students, and others can participate in the College by studying a course and also by contributing to the evolution of the software infrastructure of the Virtual College. This will provide an opportunity for students to both study and practice reuse at the same time.

Chapter 1
Introduction

During the last decade, the gap between the demand for new complex software systems and the supply has widened. This gap and the difficulties faced by software engineers in bridging it have been described as the Software Crisis, whereby systems have become so large and complex that creating software for them is increasingly more difficult to complete on time and within the constraints of the project budget. Software reuse is of growing importance as a major factor in alleviating some of the problems resulting from the Software Crisis.

The Need

Engineering is about using knowledge of natural principles from science and technology to design and build artifacts. In the early 20th century, an engineer was one who designed and supervised the execution of physical systems. In the late 20th century, the notion of engineering has been extended. For instance, *Webster's Dictionary* defines engineering as 'the application of science and mathematics by which the properties of matter and the sources of energy in nature are made useful to man in structures, machines, products, systems, and processes'. A process is not necessarily physical.

In the first 35 years of computer history the emphasis was on hardware developments, but now the emphasis has shifted more toward human concerns. As late as the mid-1950's, 90 percent of application costs were devoted to hardware, but now 90 percent of the costs are software. This reversal reflects not only the decline in hardware costs and the increase in programmer salaries, but also the recognition that systems must be carefully designed and developed to accommodate human users.

Through history there have been various applications of *programming technologies* that could be said to have caused revolutions. For instance, the Industrial Revolution was marked by such progress as the invention of the automatic loom which had instructions to form patterns in cloth. But the complex interaction between sequences of instructions and machines that marks the modern digital computer is unparalleled in the technological history of humankind.

Software is essentially a *symbolic product* and differs from the vast range of other products produced by conventional engineering techniques. Software, once designed, has no manufacturing phase and does not deteriorate, although changing environments will usually require software modifications.

Software may be systems software or applications software. Systems software serves applications software and includes compilers, editors, file management utilities, operating system facilities, and telecommunication processors. Systems software interacts with computer hardware and usually requires scheduling, sharing of resources, and effective process management. *Applications software* performs specific, real-world tasks that the user requires. For instance, software to handle payrolls, accounts receivable, and inventories are part of the applications software prevalent in business information processing. These individual application products may be integrated into a larger product, such as a management information system.

Studies have shown that reusability can significantly improve software development productivity and quality. *Productivity* increases as parts developed for previous projects can be used in current ones, saving on development time. Quality can be increased as frequently used parts have been tested and debugged in a variety of circumstances. Despite the benefits of reuse, several factors exist which seem to discourage software developers from embracing the concept of reuse. The most often cited reasons why software is not reused are (Tracz, 1988):

- a lack of tools to support a developer in trying to reuse components,
- a lack of training for developers to create reusable components and to use
- reusable components wherever possible, and

- a lack of an educational methodology and motivation (both financial and psychological) to open the eyes of developers and their management to the practical long term benefits of reuse.

That software reuse has not been widely accepted questions the suitability of existing management practices, organisational structures and technologies involved in the development of software. In short a *rethink* of software development is needed.

What is Reuse?

The distinction between use and reuse is sometimes a subtle one. We would argue that success in society is intimately linked, in the first instance, to the ability to create products and/or services that are used. The grander success occurs when what one produces becomes a critical building block in what others create—this is reuse.

The popular reuse icon (three green arrows in a cycle) is typically about decomposing natural products and incorporating them in new natural products in a cyclic way. Software can, however, be arbitrarily often copied, and software reuse should lead to new products in a spiraling way (see Figure 1.1 Reuse Spiral)

Figure 1.1–Reuse Spiral: The figure on the left shows the cycle of physical reuse whereas the software reuse spiral can lead to progressively more software from the same original software.

More rigorously, reuse is the practice of using an asset in more than one software system. An asset is any product of the software life cycle. Reuse requires the existence of a library of assets. A reuse library is a controlled collection of assets, together with the procedures and support functions required to provide the assets for reuse. Reuse typically occurs within a domain of activity or knowledge in which applications share a set of common capabilities and data.

While the terminology of assets, reuse libraries, and domains is germane to understanding the technological side of software reuse. Software reuse is also about processes that involve people. It is about learning how to do software reuse, about planning an organizations strategy for reuse, and about maintaining a process of reuse that people have been taught to follow. Reuse is also about economics.

Many people confuse reuse with use. Each has distinct, important roles in software engineering. When one eats, one obviously uses the dishes. Are the dishes being reused? They were used previously. However, these successive uses are not what is meant by reuse except in the trivial sense. A computer program invoked from a menu is being used again. However, here again this is only the trivial sense of reuse. Use is a run-time concept, while reuse is a construction-time concept (Bassett, 1997).

Run-time is the time during which a computer executes software modules. Construction time is the time during which a programmer or a computer constructs the executable or interpretable module. Construction time precedes run time.

Activities such as invoking programs means using them as is. The important properties of usability are functionality, efficiency, and ease of use. Binding is the process of assigning values to appropriate variables in a module. When done at run time, this provides the ability to vary the module's behavior. This relates to functionality and ease of use. Such run time binding, however, tends to decrease performance. Binding at construction time provides a mode of flexibility unavailable at run time.

If a person wants to take parts of a dish and make a new dish, that is a kind of reuse. In the physical world, such reuse may be very difficult. In the software world, reuse should be natural. At run time a programs data structures and basic logic can only change slightly, otherwise the program is not predictable. At construction time the data structures and logic can change in ways that would be unacceptable at run time. A reusable component has three key properties: generality, adaptability, and usability. Generality refers to how many contexts a part can be reused. Adaptability refers to how much work must be done to adapt a component for use in each context. In summary, reuse is the process of adapting a generalized component to various contexts of use.

Types of Reuse

While current management practices are not suitable for reuse-oriented development methodologies, the unsuitability is often overstated. Part of the problem is due to a blurring of the distinction between information life-cycles and development methodologies, and one often gets blamed for the shortcomings of the other (Agresti, 1986). Roughly speaking an information life-cycle is a model for organising, planning, and controlling the activities associated with software development and maintenance. For the most part, a life-cycle prescribes a division of labor, and identifies and standardises intermediary work products. A *development methodology* on the other hand specifies a notation with which to describe those work products and a process by which to arrive at those products.

Activities associated with the life-cycle involve financial and human resources. Diverting resources, both human and financial, into building a base of reusable information has a number of organisational implications, including team structures and cost imputations. In addition to the typical project team structure of information organisations, a reuse library team is needed. Minimally, the library team would be responsible for packaging and controlling the quality of what gets added to the reuse library (Prieto-Diaz and Freeman, 1987). The librarians may work closely with the project teams that develop information as those project teams both use material from the library and contribute new material to the library.

Development methodologies broadly use either generative or building blocks approaches. The *generative approach* shortens the typical information life-cycle by removing design, implementation, and testing. Developers specify the desired product in some high-level specification language. The generated information is usually correct by construction, and no testing is needed (Simos, 1988).

The building blocks approach typically incorporates:

1. statement of the problem

2. computer-based search and retrieval of building blocks

3. assessing reuse worth of retrieved blocks

4. adapting the retrieved blocks to the present need or solving the problem afresh.

Traditionally software reuse has meant the reuse of code, gathered together in subroutine libraries. The reuse of software in the form of component libraries has existed widely since the 1950s in such languages as FORTRAN. However, experience has shown that only small improvements can be achieved by simply reusing code in this way. From the documents of the software life cycle more than the code itself can and should be reused. The hope is now to widen the scope of the reuse to cover all products of the software development process, to include the components, together with their abstractions, and their associated documentation.

Domain Analysis

Recently there has been a growing interest in domain analysis and domain model 'reuse,' extending the scope of reusable information to earlier in the development life-cycle than the code stage (Mili *et al*, 1994). At this stage the software developer is able to look at the structure of a component, expressed perhaps in some formal specification method without the important concepts of the component being masked by implementation details. This method does not offer the huge productivity gains made possible by reusing a piece of code directly but has advantages. Storing components in this manner allows for the range of requirements satisfied by any component to be extended, since the items are in a simple generic form and can thus be more widely applied, allowing changes to the design to be made directly. Storing components in this manner it should be possible to reach a stage such that if a component at the program code level is a close but not exact match for a developer's desired component the developer would be able to trace back through that component's development history and find a level of abstraction at which the component is general enough to be reused.

The main problem with reuse is how to render the software items readily reusable. Domain analysis can be a fundamental step in creating real reusable components. Organisations who have conducted domain analysis prior to creating reusable components have met with greater success in software reuse.

Domain Analysis is a method for analysing a software domain by studying existing software systems, emerging technology, and the developments in terminology of the software field (Lung and Urban, 1993). In domain analysis common characteristics from similar systems are generalised, objects and operations common to all systems within the same domain are identified, and a domain model is defined to describe the relationships between the objects

Domain modelling in software reuse aims to provide a framework for the identification of objects, operations, and other structures that can be captured as reusable software concepts. Both domain expertise and expertise in design-with-reuse are used for efficient domain modelling. Whether the *domain analyst* is an expert in the domain or not, she will require access to, and experience in the use of, tools that can aid in providing an overview of the domain. Such tools and techniques have been developed in areas such as systems analysis and knowledge engineering, where the problem of domain comprehension is also a central issue.

The concepts of 'domain analysis' and 'domain modelling' are fundamental to all object-oriented approaches to software modelling. One commonly cited and well understood example of a domain is that of Mathematical Applications. The topics in this area can be modelled into classes, such as 'equations', 'set theory', 'calculus' and so on. The equations class, for example, can be subdivided into further classes, called subclasses, such as 'simultaneous equations', 'differential equations' and so on, as can the other classes. Often these subclasses too can be split further into subclasses, and so on (see Figure 1.2 Domain Analysis).

A long document that is to be read by people usually has a table of contents or an outline. This table of contents corresponds to a hierarchy of headings in the document and gives readers an overview of the contents, enabling them to find thematically-organised sections. Due to the nature of this division a well-organised outline is a ready made form of domain model. This is an example of reuse of information already contained in documents helping the reuse process.

Hypertext

Hypertext is a richly-linked, document-like information structure. It allows the reader of a document to access the information stored in it from many perceived points of view, in any order and to follow many different paths through the information. In a hypertext system, information is stored in 'chunks' which can be of any size, depending upon implementation. These chunks are called nodes, and they can be linked together to make up a document (see Figure 1.3 Hypertext Document).

Figure 1.2–Domain Analysis: The 'Domain Analyst' divides up the domain into its various classifications

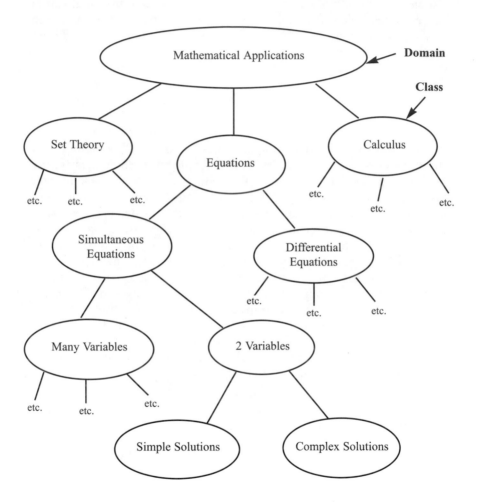

Hypertext systems are a benefit in a reuse environment because to understand a software concept that is to be reused, typically large amounts of information, which will exist for any well-documented software project, have to be examined by the developer. To access this material for relevant information by hand is tedious and time consuming. Good hypertext systems make this task easier and more accurate.

Figure 1.3–Hypertext Document: The text of the document is held in nodes, the order in which information is presented to the user will depend on the path followed through the nodes.

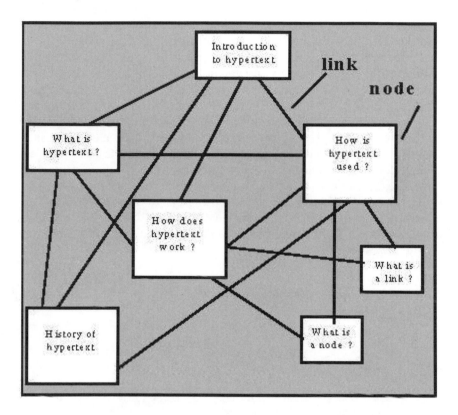

A common example of software documentation access that could be improved using hypertext is the UNIX documentation system, called 'man' (for manual). The Unix man system offers on-line documentation explaining the function and usage of programs that are available to users of the system. An example is the 'man page' for the command ls. Its 'man page' describes how to get listings of different directories and what the access rights each file is listed with mean and so on. To help the user understand what these concepts are and which commands are necessary to influence these attributes the 'man page' contains a reference to related commands.

In a hypertext system if a reference to one of these commands was present, simply clicking on the reference would retrieve the 'man page' for that command. Then clicking on another button will bring back the 'man page' from which it was summoned. This can be used recursively, if a called-up page references another page, then further references can be followed and back-tracked at will by the user.

Hypertext techniques are also useful with program code (see Figure 1.4 Ccode1). When trying to understand what a segment of code means, the developer needs to know how each of the variables in that segment are defined. The only method to find this out is usually to methodically read through the listing noting where variables are defined and modified and searching through documentation to find a description of the variable. This is tedious and with opaque code, a very difficult task. A hypertext system could automatically analyse the program to find definitions and references to variables and to search documentation for definitions. Thus, if the piece of code was being viewed using one of these systems the variables would be highlighted in some way, bold font for example, and clicking upon one of them would bring up that variable's definition and a list of references to it in the program.

Figure 1.4–Ccode1: A sample C program. The variables q1, q2, name, and buf must be understood.

```
strcpy(name,(int) q1 +2);
getblock();
q2 = (char *) strchr(buf, '"');
if (!q2)
{
        /* No luck this time */
        strcat(name,buf);
        getblock();
}
```

Hypertext may also support *collaboration*. Hypertext systems can be set to log access to each piece of information. Such a system can then keep track of who has accessed what and when. It can then be an aid to understanding which are the most important parts of the documents, who in the team understands which parts of the system, and so forth.

Epilogue

There is increasingly a need for more reliable and complex computer programs which will be delivered on time and will be cost effective to maintain. Traditional software engineering techniques do not fulfill these needs. Software reuse techniques may help.

Inhibitors to the widespread acceptance of reuse are both managerial and technological. This book emphasises a technological approach to reuse based on domain analysis and software libraries. The management problems and solutions are also described

Section 1
Background

This section provides background in the form of two chapters. The first chapter describes the software life-cycle and the second chapter introduces issues in the management of software engineers. Inhibitors to effective software reuse are largely managerial in character. Software engineers must be persuaded that creating material which fits well into a library is of long-term value. These two chapters relate to management in software engineering and to the life cycle of software components. One can not properly understand the management of the people and their tools without also understanding the processes through which the software objects themselves go. Software reuse involves many, many aspects that are both concerned with people and with software.

Chapter 2
The Software Life Cycle

The classic software life-cycle was not conceived with reuse in mind. This life-cycle has been criticized for being inherently top-down, whereas good software reuse techniques require a combination of top-down and bottom-up approaches. Nevertheless, an understanding of the traditional approach is important as a foundation for understanding reuse, and this chapter provides that foundation.

The traditional *software life-cycle* emphasizes the need for each step to meet the specifications of the previous step (see Figure 2.1 Software life-cycle). The five basic steps are:

1. Requirements describe what the client wants from the software.

2. The *design* represents the requirements in a language closer to that of the computer.

3. In the *implementation* step the design is converted into actual code that can be executed by a computer. If the design is very formalized, this may be an automatic step.

4. *Testing* is the proving of the implementation by the rigorous application of data to the system.

5. *Maintenance* is the longest part of the cycle, it is the modification of the finished program as and when the need arises.

This stage is made easier if the previous stages have been well executed.

Figure 2.1–Software life-cycle: The software life-cycle seen in a typical production engineering flow chart.

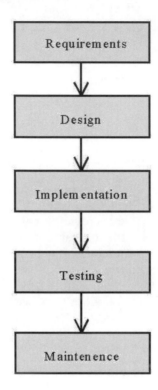

Use can also be made of other common process concepts, such as incremental delivery (Simons, 1987). In incremental delivery the software life-cycle is divided into parallel parts (see Figure 2.2 Incremental Delivery). For instance, the design can be divided into parts each of which is done separately and simultaneously but is later integrated. With rapid prototyping a simple version of the desired system is quickly constructed for the sake of insights about the important problems throughout the cycle.

Figure 2.2–Incremental Delivery: Incremental delivery view of software life-cycle.

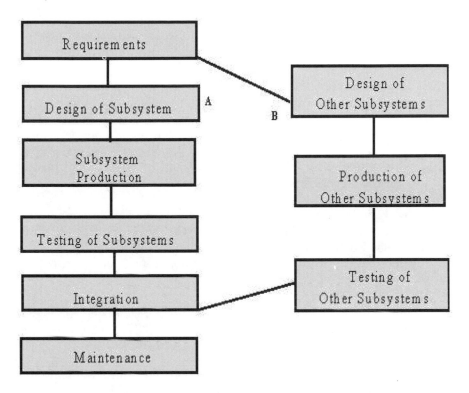

Requirements

Requirements should:

- be helpful and understandable to end users,
- serve as a basis for design and testing,
- be suitable to the application, and
- encourage thinking in terms of external and not internal system behavior.

A software requirements document establishes the first official boundaries on the solution space of the problem of developing a useful software system (Yeh and Zave, 1980). Depending on the complexity of the problem, the size of the requirements document will vary. For instance, a *requirements document* for a ballistic missile defense system contained over 8,000 requirements and filled 2,500 pages (Bell *et al*, 1977).

The most popular language for requirements is natural language because it is the most expressive and because it is understood by both users and system developers. A software requirements document contains a complete description of what the software will do without describing how it will do it. It serves as the basis for all design activities, and all system test planning. The IEEE Standards document for software quality says that requirements should (IEEE, 1981).

"clearly and precisely describe the essential functions, performances, design constraints, attributes, and external interfaces. Each requirement shall be defined such that its achievement is capable of being objectively verified by a prescribed method, for example, inspection, demonstration, analysis, or test."

While *natural language requirements* may perpetuate ambiguity, they are critically important. For example the requirements for the Ada programming environment (Defense, 1980) include:

"The database shall support the generation and control of configuration objects, that is the objects which are themselves groupings of other objects in the database."

More rigorous specifications will be needed, but they should be complemented by the natural language version, in any case. Surprisingly the expression of requirements in natural language may lead to less misunderstanding by software developers than more formal requirements.

Two major components of the requirements document are the conceptual requirements and the functional requirements. The *conceptual requirements* is a high-level description of the relationships among the services of the system. The functional requirements describe how the system will function (Yadav *et al*, 1988).

The outline of a requirements document may be divided into parts that include operational and non-operational requirements (see Figure 2.3 Operational or Testable Outline of Requirements Document). Operational or testable requirements outline the system's performance characteristics, interface constraints, quality assurance standards and human factors (Hayashi and Sekijima, 1993). The operational requirements can be traced through the design and implementation of the system. Non-operational requirements outline the organizational resources available to support system development, the package of resources available, forethoughts about the system's development cycle, assumptions about the system operation in its target environment, and expected changes in the system operational requirements over the life of the system.

Figure 2.3–Operational or Testable Outline of Requirements Document: Functional requirements detail computational functions the system is to perform. The architectural requirements describes the interconnection among abstract modules.

1. Overview

2. Problem
    2.1 Technology in use
    2.2 System diagram
    2.3 Theory of system operation
    2.4 Intended applications
    2.5 User skills

3. Operational requirements
    3.1 Performance characteristics
    3.2 Standard interfaces
    3.3 Software quality assurance
    3.4 Software portability
    3.5 User orientation

4. Non-operational requirements
    4.1 Resources available for development
    4.2 Package of resources built into system
    4.3 Forethoughts about system life cycle
    4.4 Assumptions about system operation
    4.5 Expected changes in requirements

5. Functional requirements

6. Architectural requirements

Design

Two different designers using the same design method and same requirements document would not necessarily generate the same design (though
some methodologies such as Jackson Structured Design state that they
should). The designer must still rely on his or her own insight and cre-
ativity in decomposing the system into its constituent structures and
ensuring that the design adequately captures the system specifications.
Design methods in common use have been criticized because they are
largely informal. Nevertheless they have been applied successfully in
many large projects and have resulted in significant cost reductions.

There is no single design tool which is best for all types of software
design. In fact, there are hundreds of different design tools and design
notations, each of which may be useful for describing different levels of
design within particular application areas. Some of the more common,
generic design tools include data flow diagrams, structure charts and
trees. An experiment was run in which a group of students were asked to
use various methods and a group of experts assess the results (Yadav *et
al*, 1988). The conclusion of the study was that the Data Flow Diagram
method was easier to use and learn.

Data-flow diagrams may be part of top-down design methodology.
Top-down design involves decomposing the system into its functional
sub-components and then creating a design for each sub-component. The
designs for the collection of sub-components are joined to create a design
for the overall system. For top-down design there are 4 phases:

- 1 study and understand a component of the system requirements,
- 2 identify major features of one possible design for this component,
- 3 construct a data flow diagram, showing gross data transformations in the system, and
- 4 from the data flow diagram construct a structure chart showing
  the program units, and describe these program units in pseudo-
  code.

A data flow diagram shows how data is transformed as it is moved
from one system component to another. Structure charts are hierarchical
trees with the roots at the top and are useful tools for system design. A
software system is broken down into separate programs and each program is decomposed into modules. Each of the modules is broken further

into smaller modules. Decomposition continues until the amount of information in the module is small enough to be easily managed.

By example, an Office Information Retrieval System (OIRS) can file documents under some name in one or more indices, retrieve documents, display and maintain document indices, archive documents and destroy documents. Commands might include get proposal, file as on-loan, and edit proposal. A first data flow diagram of this OIRS system reveals modules which handle each of the inputs and outputs. A further decomposition of the data flow diagram shows the user command leading into the database query. The output comes from the database and is translated into an output message and output data (see Figure 2.4 Data Flow Diagram). The structure chart takes the data flow diagram and imposes a hierarchical structure. Then it is easier to decide which effort can be independently invested in which part of the OIRS system (see Figure 2.5 Structure Chart).

Figure 2.4–Data Flow Diagram: Data flow diagram for Office Information Retrieval System. DBMS means DataBase Management System.

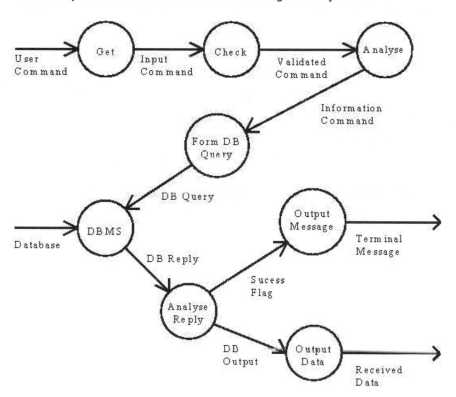

Figure 2.5–Structure Chart: Example of a structure chart for preceding Data Flow Diagram.

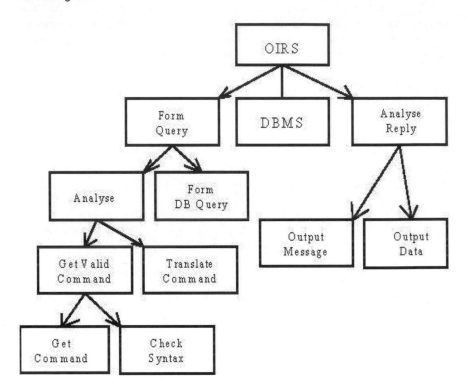

Implementation

After design comes implementation of code or software. Correspondence from design to code should be correct and traceable. It should preserve all decisions made earlier. With a well-defined design notation, it may be possible to specify explicit guidelines for mapping design constructs to code.

If a project has the opportunity to select the programming language to be used, it is desirable to consider support for high-quality, component construction provided by a candidate language. Some of the considerations include:

- Its support for extended parameterization through a facility such as Ada's generic procedures,

- Its ability to guarantee error-free, robust software through such mechanisms as type checking, and

- Its support for the creation of readable, modifiable, and maintainable programs.

Also, the anticipated language requirements of future systems should be considered.

If the programming language provides *exceptions* (a means of signaling an exceptional condition by transferring execution control to a routine specifically provided to handle that condition), this can be a way of handling boundary conditions flexibly. The component might also provide auxiliary routines for getting additional information about what caused the exception. A 'safe' component will likely include a number of checks to insure that the component does not accidentally crash. For example, there may be checks on expressions for division by zero, for checking that a queue is empty or full, or for hardware read errors when reading from a disk.

The principle of information hiding refers to the concept of making certain information visible while hiding other information. This supports the view of a 'software chip'—a black box whose function and interfaces are well-defined while no knowledge of its implementation is required. The interface specification provides the 'directions' for component installation.

In an object-oriented methodology, an object representing a data item is defined in terms of the values it holds and the operations that may take place on those values (Booch, 1994). Objects belong to *classes*, which are groups of objects which share common features, inherited from their class. The state or values held by an object are changed by sending a *message* to the object invoking one of the functions defined in it. This is a form of information hiding since the object sending the message only understands the message sent and the effect it should have, not exactly how the change will be implemented. This is useful since it means functionally equivalent objects can be swapped and when an object is reused what expectations the new program can make are clearly defined in the messages an object can receive.

Testing and Documentation

There are two main categories into which program testing strategies fall (Hartmann and Robson, 1990).

- *Functional Testing* techniques are based around checking a component using data that the component is likely to receive in use and ensuring responses are apt.

- In *Structural Testing* techniques, test data is designed using a knowledge of the structure of the component to be tested. For example, if it is known that values in the ranges 10-20, 30-40 and 80-200, will cause different branches through the program to be executed, then values in all three of these ranges would be used to test the program.

These two methods can also be combined (Woodfield *et al*, 1983).

Quality assurance or testing should not wait until code is finished. At each phase of the life-cycle, testing should ensure that the appropriate requirements for that phase are being followed. *Testing* should be included in each design review, with an established audit procedure for each product and activity. If the guidance is ignored in these early phases, little benefit will be gained from following it in the coding phase.

Testing usually focuses on products – specifications and code. These are usually amenable to objective quality measures. It is important to also audit the *work activities* that influence the quality of the product. For example, such evaluations might address:

- whether software engineering tools are being used as expected, and whether they are serving the intended purpose and

- whether changes to components are strictly controlled by configuration management procedures.

Evaluations should be objective and should be assisted by a checklist to ensure that all key points are covered. Such a checklist also provides a mechanism for documenting audit results and preparing discrepancy reports.

Documentation of the software development cycle is essential, both to manage and distribute information within the project whilst it is in progress and to be able to maintain the system once in use. In fact it can be said that the products of the software life-cycle are mainly documents. A further demonstration of this is that in 1979 within the IBM

Corporation, the title 'technical writer' was changed to 'information developer' to reflect the widening scope of the writer's responsibilities. IBM has said that information development can be thought of as one of three equal parts of a total IBM product, where the other two parts are hardware development and software development.

The authoring of documentation is called *information development* to differentiate it from normal writing activities, such as writing this book. In large organizations information development may be best accomplished within the confines of a single administrative unit. In this situation information development work can be moved within the existing organization rather than moving the information development people to different administrative units in the company. On the other hand, integrating the information developers into the overall organization increases the opportunities for synergism among the project's hardware and software groups. Differences between 'information development' and traditional technical writing include that the information developer:

- tends to get information from people rather than books,
- works as part of a team,
- tests the information for its usability, and
- may put the final written product into a variety of forms.

The information development process can be decomposed into the following sequence:

- become familiar with the hardware and software plan,
- set objectives for the information to be provided,
- develop drafts,
- verify the draft with inspection, editing, and testing, and
- maintain the information based on feedback.

The model for good information development suggests some approaches to proper education for information developers. For one, collaboration must be part of the process. For another, the hardware and software professionals must be approached as peers in the development process so that feedback can be bi-directional.

The theory of documentation stems from philosophical as well as scientific considerations and should address the broad problem of *user support technology* of which manuals are a part (Weiss, 1988). This theory should help define the relationship between internal support, such as for screen design and external support, such as manuals. It should clarify the relative costs and benefits of information services, such as teaching and consulting versus information products, such as manuals and tutorial disks. One principle of a theory of documentation is that:

> "nearly every aspect of user support (including manuals) derives from the nature of the user interface."

Consequently, the nature of the user interface must be considered as part of the initial product conception, and the user interface specification made as important as the hardware or the software specification. Another principle states that:

> "Manuals are a component in a fully-designed `user support envelope', which may include any information product or service made desirable or necessary by the user interface."

Manuals are not the lone creations of individual writers or artists. Each publication should be written to an engineered specification, not created in private by an artisan. Each part of the document should go into a data base where it will be maintained and reused by other writers. Manuals will be developed through models and prototypes and tested before they are drafted, by applying the principles to models.

Case studies reveal interesting patterns in investment in documentation. Firms which make a large investment in a product of which only a few copies are sold tend to rely heavily on personal contacts with the buyers to help the buyers use the product. Firms which sell large quantities of a modestly priced product find it cost effective to have excellent documentation because the firm could not afford the number of service calls which would be required for helping the users in person. More specifically, two variables dominate management's decision on the relative size of its investment in documentation. High projected sales volume seems to predict a relatively large investment, because high volume precludes personal contact with customers before and after sales. High unit cost, on the other hand, predicts a lower relative *investment in documentation*, because personal contact is more effective in influencing the purchase decision and competes with documentation as a means of delivering maintenance support.

In the case of low-investment documentation the vast majority of time spent on documentation goes towards writing. Relatively little time goes into management, editing, or artwork. For a high-investment documentation effort the man-months spent on each part of the documentation are relatively equally distributed among management, writing, editing, and artwork.

Maintenance

The *primary business* of the software industry has historically been new development; now it is maintenance and evolution. Today more software professionals are employed to maintain and evolve existing applications than to develop new systems from scratch. Software engineers need a variety of analytical skills, tools, and methodologies to cope with the challenges of maintaining large, aging software systems. The software industry critically depends on enhancing the maintenance processes of legacy or heritage systems which potentially constitute immense corporate advantages if managed effectively.

Every time an alteration is made to any aspect of the software, be it designs or code, it is necessary to make the corresponding change in the documentation to indicate the change. Otherwise, it may be very difficult for another programmer to understand the software sufficiently to maintain it. *Software maintenance* is the term given to the process of modifying the program after it has been delivered and is in use. These modifications may involve simple changes to correct coding errors, more extensive changes to correct design errors, or drastic rewrites to accommodate new requirements.

Programmers may hope that what is important about their programs is immediately visible. Realistically the problems are many, and cost lies under the surface. Generally the cost of software maintenance has steadily increased during the past 20 years. A typical software development organization spends about 40% - 60% of its money on software maintenance. The common error made by the maintainers is that, when an error is encountered, the coding is investigated and corrected, but the *documentation* is not correspondingly updated. Whenever a change to the software, whatever the format or type of change may be, is made, the documentation must also be updated. Otherwise a subsequent user or maintainer would find it difficult to realize the change that has been made to the original version of the software.

Standards

The importance of standards in software engineering can not be overstated. Reuse hinges on standards. A person can not reuse an object when the description is not in a language (and this means not only the natural language but also the software design language) that the person understands. The interfaces of the object to other objects have to speak the same language. If the components of the life cycle are to communicate with one another, the first standard that is required is directed to the commonality in the language that is used to describe the software life cycle. This chapter has summarized some of the key views on and components of the software life cycle. Next standards for the software life cycle are considered after an introductory look at standards organizations and processes.

The standard making process involves many different groups whose mode of operation is a complex combination of commerce and government. Consensus must be obtained and often this involves significant expenditure of resources in time and money. An advanced country tends to have at least one major standards institute. The United States has the American National Standards Institute, the United Kingdom has the British Standards Institute, and so on. An alliance of European nations has created a standards organization called the Committee of European Normalization which receives input from 18 European countries. The International Organization for Standards receives input from virtually all countries. In addition to the national and supranational organizations, many commercial and volunteer groups play important roles in developing standards (Rada *et al*, 1994). For instance, the Institute of Electrical and Electronic Engineers (IEEE) sponsors the development of numerous standards.

The International Organization of Standards (ISO) is an independent organization for fostering international agreement on standards with a view to expanding international trade. ISO consists of national representatives only. The work of ISO is undertaken by Technical Committees. A draft standard is advanced by a Technical Committee to the membership of ISO, and if 75% of the membership of ISO approve, then the draft becomes an International Standard.

American Standards

Traditionally, each sector interested in regulating the development and maintenance of software has written its own specification to summarize the requirements of interest. Over twenty years ago the U.S. government over twenty years ago organized a software life cycle around ten documents (NBS, 1976). At roughly the same time, the U.S. Navy commissioned a standard for the software life cycle (USN, 1976). The Federal Aviation Authority and other regulatory bodies also standardized the software life cycle they expected contractors to follow in developing quality software.

The commercial sector also helped to proliferate life cycle standards. The Institute of Electrical and Electronic Engineers (IEEE) created a standard for the definition of life cycle processes, IEEE Std 1074. Unlike the aforementioned standards which placed requirements on the external characteristics of a life cycle, 1074 focused on the life cycle model. It specified a number of process fragments along with their inputs and outputs. The process architect could assemble a life cycle model from the pieces specified by the standard. Even private companies, like IBM, had their own life cycle definitions, treated as proprietary material because they were presumed to confer a competitive advantage.

If the 1970s and 80s were a period of differentiation in life cycle standards, the 1990s were a period of consolidation. The DoD undertook an effort to unify various software life cycle standards it had sponsored. The IEEE and the Electronics Industry Association then produced a joint standard that the American National Standards Institute (ANSI) issued as ANSI Joint Standard 016.

ISO 12207

While each country was developing its own software life cycle standards, the international standards community was also active. ISO/IEC JTC1/SC7 (the software engineering subcommittee of Joint Technical Committee 1 of the International Organization for Standardization and the International Electrotechnical Commission) developed a standard known as ISO/IEC 12207. Whereas ANSI 016 placed requirements on only the development process, 12207 specified four additional primary processes (acquisition, supply, maintenance, and operation), as well as eight supporting processes and four organizational processes. Although 12207 is useful in organizational or individual contexts, its conformance requirement specifically applies to the relationship between an acquirer and a supplier in the development, maintenance, or operation of software. The standard is intended to be tailored by the deletion of inapplicable tasks (specific parts of processes) when it is applied to any particular contract. (Of course, additional requirements may be placed in a contract.) On the other hand, organizations that adopt the standard as a "condition of trade" are expected to publish the minimum set of acceptable tasks.

ISO 12207 impacts international commerce in software because it provides a common framework of terminology and process structure for acquirers and suppliers in different countries. Many of the major countries are moving toward the adoption of 12207 as a national standard. Nevertheless, there are some obstacles to use, particularly by U.S. users. The standard does not provide a set of data descriptions for the recording of information essential to software development. The standard provides no way for an organization to assert that its own internally institutionalized software development methods conform to 12207. The standard does not provide a clear transition path for the large number of U.S. stakeholders in the ANSI-016 and related standards.

The various national U.S. bodies have created a "U.S. Industrial Implementation" of 12207. Recall that organizations can tailor ISO 12207 and augment it with material from ANSI 016 and other sources. IEEE has adopted 12207 "as is". IEEE has mapped some of its many standards to the ISO 12207 framework (see Figure 2.6 IEEE and ISO). U.S. efforts have developed an "organizational" mode that permits an organization to assert that its internally adopted processes for software development, maintenance, or operation me*et al*l of the requirements of the U.S. 12207—a 12207 badge.

Figure 2.6–IEEE and ISO: Existing IEEE Standards support the ISO 12207 Process Framework. The leftmost column is the high-level process addressed by ISO 12207, while the second column is the next-level process in ISO 12207. The third column is an IEEE standard that relates directly to the corresponding ISO process.

ISO 12207 Process		Corresponding IEEE SESC Standard
Primary	Acquisition	1062 Software Acquisition
	Development	830 Software Requirements Specifications, 1016 Software Design Descriptions, 1008 Software Unit Testing
	Maintenance	1219 Software Maintenance
Supporting	Configuration Management	828 Software Configuration Management Plans
	Quality Assurance	730 Software Quality Assurance Plans
	Verification	1012 Software Verification and Validation

Figure 2.6–IEEE and ISO, con't

ISO 12207 Process		Corresponding IEEE SESC Standard
	Joint Review	1028 Software Reviews and Audits
	Problem Resolution	1044 Classification of Software Anomalies
Organizational	Management	1058 Software Project Management Plans
	Infrastructure	1209 Evaluation and Selection of CASE Tools
Tailoring		1074 Developing Software Life Cycle Processes

A 12207 badge suits the needs of the U.S. defense industry, one of the primary customers of software engineering standards. When the Department of Defense stopped writing and imposing its own process standards, it endorsed the concept that contractors should develop their own organizational processes conforming to generally accepted standards. Defense contractors are among the first to display the 12207 badge. ISO is exploiting the success of 12207 in several ways. A guidebook providing advice on 12207 usage is available. ISO is reshaping its other software engineering standards projects so they will "plug into" the 12207 life cycle processes.

Process Assessment Methods

A badge already familiar to some U.S. software developers is the Capability Maturity Model developed by the Software Engineering Institute at Carnegie-Mellon University. The CMM began as a self-assessment mechanism intended to guide the improvement of organizational software development processes. It grew to an evaluation mechanism, applied by some agencies of the U.S. Department of Defense to judge the capabilities of potential suppliers.

U.S. software developers may not be as familiar with assessment models and methods, such as Trillium (Bell, 1994), Bootstrap and perhaps a half-dozen others, developed by organizations in other countries. The proliferation of assessment mechanisms presents a barrier to organizations desiring to act as suppliers in the international software marketplace.

To address these concerns, ISO/IEC JTC1 created in 1993, a project called SPICE (Software Process Improvement and Capability dEtermination) assigning it to SC7, the same subcommittee that developed the 12207 standard. The objective of the SPICE project is to harmonize existing process assessment approaches by identifying a common framework. Work to date suggests a two-dimensional framework: one dimension structured by the processes of 12207; the other dimension structured similarly to maturity levels. The framework would be applicable to assessing process capability within an organization as well as determining the capability of potential suppliers. It is intended that the standard would be culturally independent and applicable to a variety of application domains and organizations.

The intent is to allow users of existing models to continue their use while providing a common framework against which results of the various models and methods can be reported and tracked. Whether organizations wear a badge saying "SPICE" or a badge bearing a more familiar name, it seems likely that process assessment will be applied on an international scale.

IEEE's Customer-Oriented Program

The IEEE *Software Engineering Standards Committee* (SESC) is the world's most prolific creator of software engineering practice standards. Its collection numbers over 35 and grows at the rate of five or so per year. Organizations that apply the SESC standards do so without compulsion.

One reason to adopt the SESC standards is that the collection represents a comprehensive corpus of practices for good software engineering. Furthermore, some organizations find themselves in the unenviable position of defending their development practices in regulatory or legal situations. Their defense might be to say that they have applied a recognized body of software engineering practice, the SESC collection. For example, a major consumer credit reporting company, sued for alleged reckless conduct in the development of its databases and software, has adopted the entire collection to defend itself against future court challenges. A utility company applies the standards to the development of nuclear plant operating software and performs causal analysis all the way to the standards themselves whenever a fault is discovered.

Despite such successes, the SESC collection does have its problems. Accreted in a piece-wise fashion over twenty years, the collection has legitimately been criticized as ad hoc. Beginning in 1993, the SESC began a re-organization of its standards to address these concerns and to ensure that their collection of standards was responsive to the needs of their customers—software engineers. The strategic plan is captured in several key documents:

- The SESC Survey identified 220 existing and in-progress normative documents developed by 46 organizations on the subject of software engineering (Magee and Tripp, 1994).

- The SESC Master Plan identified 18 classes of customers for software engineering standards and enumerated a set of expectations, a total of 370 of them, for each class of customers. It specified 165 objectives for software engineering standards, allocated to 26 subject areas. It listed 58 general requirements and constraints on those standards and postulates 222 topics for potential standards.

- Their SESC 1995 Strategy Statement placed software engineering within the context of the related disciplines of quality management and systems engineering, including cross-cutting disciplines such as safety and dependability.

The SESC Strategy Plan adopted a unified organizational idiom for all of the SESC standards: any standard is applied by a project; a project interacts with a customer, uses resources, and executes processes to produce products (IEEE, 1995). These four items of customer, resources, processes, and products form the program elements for a reorganized collection of software engineering standards. Each program element will be packaged as a unified collection, including top-level policies and principles, key element standards, and accompanying guides all drawing on a shared toolbox of technique standards. The entire collection will be unified with a single terminology standard and an overall road map that will also position the SESC collection with respect to the relevant international standards.

SESC's work is coordinated with that of ISO/IEC JTC1/SC7 through the ANSI Technical Advisory Group to SC7. This coordination suggests that one possible result is a revision of the SESC collection so that a core group of standards can be directly applied to add detail to the process framework of 12207 (see again Figure 2.6 "IEEE and SESC" for the close fit that already exists). Under legal and regulatory pressure, some organizations already wear the badge of conformance to the SESC collection of standards. Earning that badge will become more attractive to a wider variety of organizations as the various coordinated standards become available. SESC will thus help connect ISO 12207 and SPICE. Organizations may eventually be expected to wear the 12207 badge (to signify adoption of the international life cycle process framework), to wear the SESC badge (to signify adoption of standards detailing the 12207 processes), and to wear the SPICE badge (to signify maturity in applying those processes).

Epilogue

Reuse may take place at any level of the life-cycle model, and thus the model needs to be addressed at each level to reflect reuse practices. Perhaps one of the most fundamental criticisms of the traditional software life cycle is its separation of design and implementation. In a reuse environment, design and implementation are linked. To implement with a pre-designed (reusable) component may mean going back and changing the design. Analysts may need to look ahead in the process to determine what components are available to them in the components library and tailor their design accordingly. It would therefore be better, if these two stages were linked.

Reuse of components is greatly facilitated if the components are in machine-readable form. This is essential for effective computer organization and retrieval of the material (which is discussed later in this book) and also means that the components can be loaded into software engineering support tools, since this will usually facilitate the easiest manipulation of this material. This portability of representations is unlikely to be generally possible until there are more widespread standards for these representations and tools.

The plethora of existing software life cycle models and languages is one barrier to reuse. At least, within a given domain such as manufacturing software or health care software, software engineering organizations in that discipline need to agree on some standards. This agreement on standards is a salient mark of a profession. This conformance to the standards will be associated with badges. Software product and service providers will earn and wear these badges to signify their compliance with professional standards.

Chapter 3
Management

Developing large software systems must be treated, at least in part, as a learning, communicating and negotiating process. At the early phases of a project much of the effort must go into becoming familiar with the application. A small subset of the design team with superior application knowledge often exerts a large impact on the design. Organizational boundaries to communication among groups inhibit the integration of existing knowledge. Any software development environment must become a medium of communication. This chapter describes the role of communication in team organization and in project modeling and scheduling.

Software Team Organization

The popular image of programmers is that they work alone, an image held both by the programmers themselves and others. In fact, a great deal of programming is cooperative. In one major study 50% of a typical programmer's time was spent interacting with other team members, 30% working alone, and 20% in not directly productive activities (McCue, 1978). The interaction of personalities within a group and the role of the leader are critical to group success.

Experience suggests that programming teams should be relatively small—fewer than 9 members (Sommerville, 1996). A small team minimizes communication problems, supports consensus management, and allows each member to know what each other member is doing. If one person leaves, that person's work can be easily continued. High-level system design is done by senior team members but low-level design is the responsibility of the person given the task. A serious problem arises when no team members have substantial experience, for then the authority of the experienced members is missing and coordination suffers.

Figure 3.1–Hierarchical Management: Sketch of part of hierarchy in information technology management.

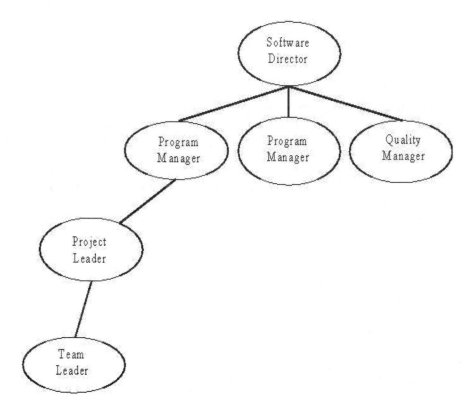

The traditional *management structure* is strictly hierarchical (see Figure 3.1 Hierarchical Management). In a large organization there should be a director of software or information technology. This person may well have vice-president status in the organization. Reporting to this director are several program managers and a quality manager. The quality manager also has several teams of quality assurance people whose job is to help evaluate the success of the software development which is being directed by the other program managers. The quality manager has a direct line to the director so as to avoid distortion of the quality assessment results. The program managers have project managers who report to them, and team leaders report to the project managers.

The *chief programmer* team approach utilizes an experienced chief programmer and provides him with substantial support (Baker, 1972). All communication goes through the team chief. The other members of the team might include :

- Backup programmer who provides general support as well as developing test cases,
- Librarian who does all clerical work associated with the project and is assisted by a computerized document management system,
- Toolsmith who produces software tools,
- Documentation editor who prepares the documentation of the chief programmer for publication,
- Project administrator who does administrative tasks for the chief programmer, and
- Language and system expert who is familiar with the idiosyncrasies of the language and system and helps the chief programmer take advantage of those idiosyncrasies.

A diagram of the 'chief programmer' concept shows the relative decentralization that the concept allows relative to the traditional approach where a programmer is at the bottom of a large hierarchy of administrators (see Figure 3.2 Chief Programmer).

The technical and the administrative leader of a software group are not necessarily the same person. Expertise with the technology and handling the problem at hand is so important in programming work that the person with this expertise at any given point is likely to command respect. The autocratic style of leadership which may suit the military does not necessarily suit programming groups. Group loyalty can be important in that it strengthens the interpersonal ties and makes it easier for people to help one another. On the other hand, the group leader must prevent a group from adopting narrow-minded attitudes as a consequence of the conservative impacts of loyalty.

Figure 3.2–Chief Programmer: The Chief Programmer paradigm allows the expert programmer to take advantage of the resources of a team of assistants.

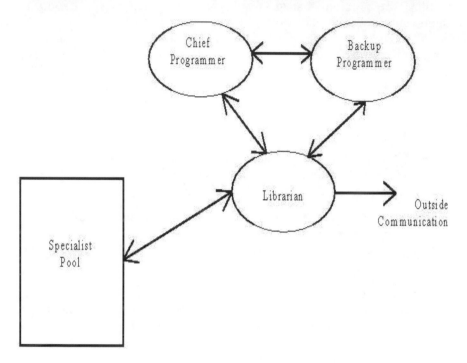

Individuals in a work situation can be classified into three types. An individual type and what motivates that type are paired as follows:

- the *task-oriented* type is interested primarily in the work,
- the *interaction-oriented* type of person most appreciates the presence of co-workers, and
- the individual wants mainly personal success.

When a group was composed entirely of members of one type, only the group composed of interaction-oriented individuals succeeded. The most successful groups have individuals from each class with the leader being task-oriented. In practice, two group members often play complementary roles. A task specialist sets, allocates, and coordinates the work of the group. An interaction specialist helps maintain the social equilibrium of the group (Weinberg, 1971). Since the majority of those involved in computer programming work are task-oriented, attention must be paid to the selection of members of a group to assure a mixture of personality types. Egoless programming requires the members of a group to contribute to the group without necessarily identifying the productivity of individuals. In this way, an individual is less likely to feel attacked when criticisms arise about work which that individual produced.

While communication is critical for group productivity, communication is often not directly productive. Accordingly, a group should be organized so that the amount of communication necessary for effectiveness is minimized. One way to do this is to have a small group. The layout of the office space should allow privacy on the one hand and group face-to-face meetings of both a formal and informal nature. In other words, the individual should have a private space with his or her own workstation, but a lounge should be available for informal meetings, and a seminar room should be available for group meetings.

Process Modeling

Reuse can occur on more than code, it can occur on process models of an organization. These models were discussed loosely in the preceding section. Here, one particular method and language for developing such process models is presented. Activity standards are prescribed in places, such as ISO 12207 (see the preceding chapter), but process model for a particular organization must include and thus transcend just the activity models.

Software reuse has gone further and further from the emphasis on simply reusing code to the emphasis on appreciating and reusing information throughout the software life cycle. This has corresponded with an appreciation of the importance of describing the entire organizational operation and reusing that information as well (Cockburn, 1996). This higher level analysis of activities in an organization may go under the heading of patterns work and an issue of the Communications of the ACM was devoted to such patterns in 1996 (Schmidt, *et al*, 1996).

A simple taxonomy of business process models distinguishes formal methods from empirical ones. The object-oriented paradigm used here is empirical. The modeling language is called Gertrude (Succi *et al*, 1997) and uses four entities: people, roles, processes, and infrastructures. People fill roles. Roles execute processes through activity profiles of the roles and processes. Infrastructure provides materials for processes.

Activities are atomic processes. People are the employees of the firm; they play roles to perform the activities. Infrastructures are passive physical objects, such as equipment and facilities. A process may be further categorized as interfacing to roles and infrastructure outside the firm or inside to controlling other processes, or to neither interfacing nor controlling.

As employees in the firm must benefit from the model, they need to understand the modeling language to some extent. The modeler has to know the details of the language. Other people may be given external views that hide complexities or details of the model and its language so that those people can derive from the model just what they need to know.

To do quantitative evaluations, such as productivity and profitability, activity-based costing is incorporated in the Gertrude approach. When a process is executed, data is collected about resource consumption. If a process is reused with changes, it is necessary to evaluate the effects of the changes on the profitability of the process.

The modeling process is approached in an iterative fashion both off-line and on-line. Off-line means by benefiting from accumulated information. On-line means the firm provides data on a day-to-day basis that is directly incorporated in the model building.

An example of the modeling is presented. Employees describe the operations in the firm. Some general patterns appear. For instance, a verbal description like this might appear:

> The client asks for a design. Sue handles the order and requirements. Sue informs John about the resource requirements. John uses a resource-allocation strategy to choose which designers will handle the project. The designers work on the project. The design is passed to Ann who meets with the client to discuss the designs suitability. Ann then reports to John on the success of the design, and John determines the next step in resource allocation.

In this process, four activities have been identified:

- interaction with client,
- resource allocation,
- design, and
- validation.

Roles have also been identified within a hierarchy to include at the bottom manager, designer, and analyst (see Figure 3.3 Roles Hierarchy). In this approach, people have no intrinsic hierarchical relation among themselves, but only to the extent they assume roles in the hierarchy are they associated with reporting relations. A process hierarchy is also developed in which design and validation are both grouped under development processes because of their cost and value similarity.

Figure 3.3–Roles Hierarchy: The boxes describe roles. The lines indicate taxonomy hierarchical relations.

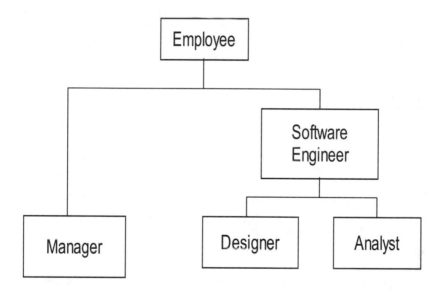

Activity-based costing forms are distributed to employees who keep track of their investments of time and other resources on each activity to which their role(s) commit. As a result of these recordings, John, the resource manager, notes that one of the designers is taking much longer than expected. Accordingly, a new activity is added to the firm's list of things to do, namely to evaluate the possible value of computer-aided design tools for the designer in question. The Gertrude model of the firm is then updated to incorporate this request for computer-aided design tool assessment.

Software Project Modeling

Many models for costing software projects have been developed. In one experiment several of these models were applied to the same input data, but cost estimates were produced which varied from $300,000 to $3,000,000 (Mohanty, 1981). This vast discrepancy points to the importance of choosing a model which fits the character of the organization and project at hand. One of the better documented software costing models is the COCOMO one (Boehm, 1981). The COCOMO (COnstructive COst MOdel) method is based on the premise that one can estimate the number of thousand (or Kilo) Delivered Source Instructions (KDSI) that will be needed to complete a project. This quantity is then used to compute an estimate for the effort required for completing that project. Estimating KDSI may be as difficult as estimating the effort directly. However, by breaking the system into small enough modules, one can estimate the KDSI for each module. Then assuming that interactions among modules will not lead to significant additional needed instructions, the total KDSI is the sum of the KDSI over the modules.

Versions of the estimation formula exist for both organic mode projects and embedded mode projects. An organic mode project requires only a small team working in a familiar environment. Communications overhead is low. An embedded mode project involves a maze of hardware, software, and regulations. Project team members are new to this problem type, this is a more complex problem and the completion time will be correspondingly longer. Even though the output of the COCOMO model is very rough, it can be useful for management decision making. Graphically, the relationship of person-months to KDSI is like a straight line for the organic form and a parabola for the embedded form (see Figure 3.4 COCOMO Curves).

The simple assumption about effort is that the amount expended on a project is proportional to the product of the number of people working on a project and the amount of time they spend on the project. Thus, if each of 10 people works 5 days on a project, then the project has had 50 *person-days* invested into it. Assessing projects as to the number of person-days required to complete them implies that assigning more people to a task would shorten the number of days required to complete the project. For instance, 50 people working one day might be able to solve the 50 person-day problem. In reality, however, this assumption about productivity is misleading. The difficulty is akin to the difficulty with multiple processors in a parallel-processing computer. Namely, as more processors are assigned to a task, the inter-processor communication costs rise and may overwhelm the advantage of additional processing power.

Figure 3.4–COCOMO Curves: Curves showing the growth in person-months needed to generate a certain number of lines of code.

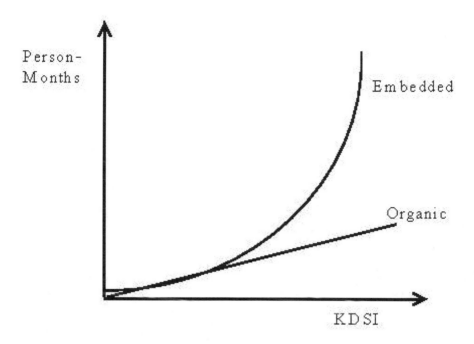

Each new person brought into a project needs instructions about what he or she is to do, which takes time from those who give the instructions. The new person can do work but also needs guidance which costs the work time of others. In the worst case, the *communication needs* are such that a new person must communicate with every person already on the project. If there are p-people and each must spend time in contact with the other p-1 people, then the amount of contact is p(p-1) or roughly p^2. The effort which can be expended by p people over t time when there is no overhead cost is p times t. Given that e effort satisfies e = p times t, the time to complete a given task is t = e over p. As p grows, t declines. If the communication costs are considered, then these costs are proportional to the square of the number of people. In this case, the curve of t versus p no longer declines monotonically with p; rather there is an inflection point from which t rises with rising p (see Figure 3.5 Time Rising).

Figure 3.5–Time Rising: Curve showing the initial decline but the subsequent rise in time as people are added to the job.

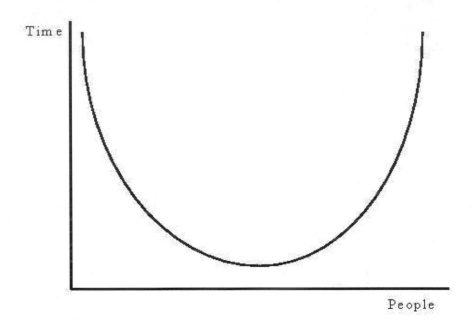

Scheduling

Without some estimate of *programmer productivity*, project scheduling is impossible. Also, some of the advantages to the use of new programming and management methodologies are difficult to assess without quantitative measures of programmer productivity. The most commonly used measure of programmer productivity is lines of source code per programmer-month. This is computed by dividing the number of lines of source code delivered by the programmer-months in the project. The programmer-months include analysis and design, coding, testing, and documentation time. One of the difficulties in applying this measure of productivity is defining 'a line of code' (Jones, 1978) Another difficulty is that this measure does not take into account the quality of the code produced, only the quantity.

Figure 3.6–Bar Chart: Person A does tasks T1, T2, and T4, while Person B does tasks T3 and T5.

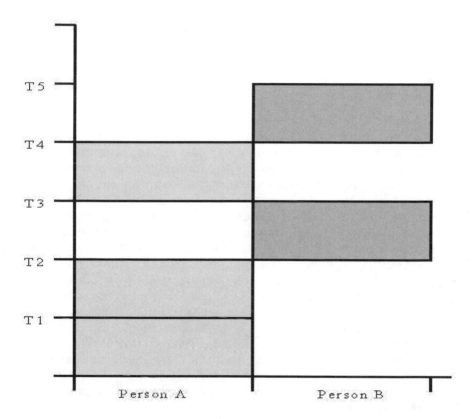

There are a number of different tools available to help schedule projects. While bar charts provide a useful visualization of part of project planning, they fail to show dependencies among tasks. For instance, if T3 has to be done before T4, then a delay in the completion of T3 must be reflected in a change in the timing of T4 (see Figure 3.6 Bar Chart). Activity networks overcome this deficiency, as they portray dependencies. Each node of an activity graph represents the culmination of one or more activities. A labeled arc from one node to another could represent the name of the activity along with the time required to complete the activity.

To develop a schedule, a project is first broken down into tasks. Next one asks: 'What other tasks must be completed before this task finishes ?' 'How long will it take to perform this particular task ?' Given a project begin time, one can compute the 'Earliest Begin' and the 'Earliest Finish' times for each task, and the total project duration.

Epilogue

Producing large systems is a difficult task of managing both people and information. This is true in a reuse environment where extra personnel, such as those that manage and retrieve elements from the reuse library, are needed. The Chief programmer approach to software team organization includes reuse-oriented roles, such as the librarian role.

Of the many models which have been developed to model the development of software systems, the COCOMO model is perhaps the best known. It estimates the number of lines of code that a project will need to produce and shows interesting relations among project type and effort required. Reuse parameters can be folded into the COCOMO model.

The mythical man-month notion (Brooks, 1975) shows that adding more people to a project does not necessarily reduce the time needed to finish the project. Adding a person to the project may bring more communication costs than productivity benefits. Initiating a reuse effort may initially require additional staff and their concomitant costs.

To schedule a software project, tasks and their dependencies must be appreciated. Software reuse introduces new tasks and dependencies. The challenge then is to manage these dependencies so that overall benefit exceeds overall cost.

Section 2
Enterprise and
Standards

This section contains two chapters. The first details a conceptual framework for reuse. A reuse life cycle for software assets is described that centers around the library of assets. The human issues in the reuse framework are also emphasized in a cycle of activity that goes from planning to enactment to learning. The enterprise chapter also addresses economics and legal issues. Software reuse involves many, many aspects that are both concerned with people and with software. For instance, to establish a software reuse library one should first estimate the costs of developing software with or without the library. Legal matters, such as copyright, may play an important role in determining what is or is not reused.

The second chapter of this section looks at standards relevant to reuse. Reuse in some fundamental ways requires standardization. People have to agree on the language of discourse, assets have to be able to communicate with other assets through standard interfaces, and organizations must communicate in clear, systematic ways to their employees about processes for reuse. Certainly, standards within an organization exist but these are being supported increasingly by formal, global standards, and those are the subjects of the second chapter in this Section.

Chapter 4
Reuse Framework

The *vision for reuse* is to move from the current 're-invent the software' cycle to a library-based way of constructing software (DoD, 1992). A conceptual framework for reuse should provide the technological and management basis to influence and enable this paradigm shift. In this new paradigm the standard approach to software development is to derive systems principally from existing assets rather than to create the systems anew. Reusable assets are thus a central concept of the reuse vision, and they imply a need for processes to create such assets, manage them and utilize them to produce new systems.

Experience suggests that this library-based approach must be domain-specific. *Being domain-specific* means that the reusable assets, the development processes, and the supporting technology are appropriate to the application domain for which the software is being developed. Application domains are generally considered to be broad in scope, for example communication systems. The effectiveness of domain-specific assets depends on a number of factors, including the maturity of the application domain and the investment applied to create the assets. As a domain matures, it generally becomes more stable and better understood, thus increasing the likelihood that assets will be reusable. However, even in mature domains, asset reusability and quality will be maximized only if suitable investment has been applied to identify and exploit key reuse opportunities. Domain analysis and its resultant models are critical to the success of a domain-specific reuse program.

Process Idioms and Sources

Software engineering should be done in accordance with well defined, repeatable processes. One framework for reuse consists of dual, interconnected 'process idioms' called Reuse Management and Reuse Engineering (see Figure 4.1 Reuse Management and Reuse Engineering). Outputs from the Framework are software systems and new reusable assets.

Figure 4.1–Reuse Management and Reuse Engineering: Plan, Enact, and Learn are in the Management idiom. Create, Manage and Utilize are in the Engineering idiom.

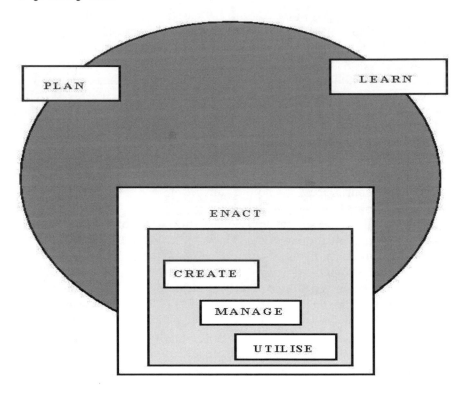

The *Reuse Management* idiom describes a cyclic pattern of activity addressing the establishment and continual improvement of reuse-oriented activities within an organization by emphasizing learning as an institutional mechanism for change. Learning in this context means actively evaluating and reflecting on behavior to effect positive change. The Reuse Engineering idiom also explicitly recognizes the role of the broker as a mediator between asset producers and consumers. The Reuse Management and Reuse Engineering idioms represent reuse-specific adaptations of more general forms of organizational activity. The Framework specializes these more general idioms to facilitate adaptation of a wide body of management and organizational theory to the software reuse problem.

The Framework is *generic* with respect to domains, organizations, and technologies. Framework concepts should generally be applicable to reuse in any information-intensive context, such as technical documentation or scientific information management. The scope is limited to identifying the processes involved in reuse and describing at a high level how those processes operate and interact.

The Framework which is described in this chapter is largely based on a document entitled "STARS Conceptual Framework for Reuse Processes" (Boeing, 1993). That document reflects an effort to modernize software productivity by the *Software Technology* for *Adaptable, Reliable Systems* (STARS) program of the U.S. Department of Defense. The Framework reflects the experiences of software reuse efforts both within and outside of STARS. The Framework provides a conceptual foundation for reuse processes needed to accomplish the STARS reuse mission. However, for an organization undertaking a reuse program, the Framework must be augmented and numerous documents provide information for such an augmentation (STARS, 1993; 1993b; Virginia, 1992; Frakes and Gandel, 1990)

Naturally, other organizations also have reuse frameworks. For instance, the North Atlantic Treaty Organization has published a 3-volume standard for software reuse (GTE, 1992a, 1992b, 1992c). The volumes are entitled:

- Development of Reusable Software Components,
- Management of a Reusable Software Component Library, and
- Software Reuse Procedures.

The content of these 3 volumes is in principle harmonious with the content of the 'Conceptual Framework for Reuse' of STARS.

Figure 4.2–Reuse Management: Planning, Enacting, and Learning include the processes.

REUSE MANAGEMENT
- Planning
  Assessment
  Direction Setting
  Scoping
  Infrastructure Planning
  Project Planning

- Enacting
  Project Management
  Infrastructure Implementation

- Learning
  Project Observation
  Project Evaluation
  Innovation Exploration
  Enhancement Recommendation

Reuse Management

Reuse involves both people and information. The Reuse Management process idiom focuses on people. It describes a cyclical pattern of planning, enacting, and learning (see Figure 4.2 Reuse Management). Reuse Management incorporates emerging general theories of organizational learning (Senge, 1990) that have been adapted to the reuse-based software engineering context. The following subsections deal with managing people, but later this chapter will emphasize the information-side of reuse under the headings of Asset Creation, Asset Management, and Asset Utilization.

Reuse Planning

The *Reuse Planning* process encompasses both strategic planning and tactical, project-oriented planning within a reuse program. One key strategic reuse planning function, which augments traditional product line planning within an organization, is to select the key domains of focus for the reuse program and determine how the domain assets will support the organization's product engineering efforts. One key focus of Reuse Planning is the reuse infrastructure that is required to sustain a reuse-based software engineering approach. The outputs from the reuse Planning family include:

- Plans for the reuse program, and
- Committed resources to support the projects, in terms of staff and equipment.

The five processes in planning are Assessment, Direction Setting, Scoping, Infrastructure Planning, and Project Planning.

1. Assessment processes characterize the current state of reuse practice within an organization, the readiness of the organization as a whole for practicing reuse-based software engineering, and the reuse technology and expertise available.
2. Direction Setting processes define specific objectives for the reuse program, strategies for achieving those objectives, and criteria for evaluating how successfully the objectives have been met.
3. Scoping processes define the overall scope of the reuse program by delineating the program's technical and organizational boundaries. The technical scope is defined in terms of the domains and product lines to be encompassed by the reuse program, while the organizational scope is defined in terms of the program's organizational context and management influence.

A first step in domain selection is to identify and characterize promising candidate domains, based on the organization's business interests, key areas of expertise, and existing legacy systems. Criteria for identifying promising domains include (Holibaugh, *et al*, 1989):

- The domain is well-understood, and
- The domain is based on predictable technology that will not make the reusable assets obsolete before the investment in their development can be recovered.

4. Infrastructure Planning processes identify needs for various types of support that are common among planned reuse projects, and develop plans for establishing a shared reuse infrastructure to satisfy those needs.
5. Project Planning processes plan the reuse program's Reuse Engineering projects in detail. Project Planning is responsible for

establishing specific objectives for each identified project, and for defining the metrics to be used to evaluate the effectiveness of the projects relative to those objectives. A variety of metrics can be defined relating specifically to assets and reuse, such as:

- The percentage of each application product that was directly derived from domain assets,
- The number of times each asset has been reused, and
- The number of regular users of an asset library.

The final stage of Project Planning is to plan the reuse project's resource needs, budgets, and schedules in detail and then obtain the necessary commitment to implement the plans. Commitment should be obtained from both higher level management and the technical staff members whose buy-in will ultimately determine whether or not reuse practice is really improved by the program.

Reuse Enactment and Reuse Learning

Reuse Enactment addresses initiation, performance, and retirement of the various reuse-related plans. *Reuse Enactment* includes Project Management processes and Infrastructure Implementation processes. *Project Management processes* establish a temporal context for reuse project activities and include the following specific functional areas:

- Project initiation activities include allocation and tailoring of technical reuse infrastructure capabilities to specific projects.
- Project performance is where the processes being enacted are actually performed by individual staff members.
- Project control activities intervene with project performance to optimize overall project performance relative to project objectives.
- Project monitoring activities capture information from the projects as they are performed.
- Project retirement activities include terminating the project and archiving the key results.

Infrastructure Implementation processes ensure that reuse infrastructure capabilities are established and evolved in accordance with project needs.

The goal of Reuse Learning processes is to enhance the performance of a reuse program. The results of Reuse Learning are fed back to Reuse Planning processes in the form of recommendations for the next reuse program cycle. Reuse Learning includes Project Observation and Innovation Exploration processes.

Project Observation processes gather information about enacted reuse projects. A primary goal of Reuse Learning processes is to support the evolution of an organization's reuse-based software engineering capabilities. *Innovation Exploration processes* address this goal in a different way than Project Evaluation, by gathering, generating, analyzing, and testing new ideas, discoveries, and innovations to generate recommendations for major improvements.

Asset Creation

Reuse Engineering addresses the creation, management, and utilization of reusable assets. Asset Management serves a brokerage role between Asset Creation and Asset Utilization and reflects common marketplace interactions (see Figure 4.3 Decomposition of Reuse Engineering). In an organization that has a mature reuse program underway, there will likely be multiple Asset Creation, Asset Management, and Asset Utilization projects in operation simultaneously.

The goals of *Asset Creation* are to capture, organize, and represent knowledge about a domain, and use that knowledge to develop reusable assets. Asset Creation can be viewed as consisting of:

- 1 Domain Modeling processes that characterize application products in terms of what the products have in common and how they vary, and

- 2 Asset Implementation processes that produce reusable assets.

Domain models and asset bases are logically at different levels of abstraction and serve different purposes. The primary role of domain models within Asset Creation is to assist in determining which asset should be produced and the range of characteristics they should support. For that reason, domain models focus on describing the commonality and variability among systems, rather than on describing the systems themselves. The assets that are developed using the domain models are at a lower level of abstraction, they implement products.

Although there are many domain analysis methods (e.g.,, STARS, 1993b; DISA, 1993), there remains little consensus on specific techniques. However, many existing *domain analysis processes* have in common the following general activities:

- Reverse engineering,
- Knowledge acquisition,
- Technology forecasting,
- Domain modeling, and
- Asset specification.

To extract expertise already encoded in legacy systems, they are often analyzed using reverse engineering techniques. Processes to support knowledge acquisition in domain analysis can be adapted from knowledge acquisition techniques used for in-depth interviewing in any discipline.

In order for reuse to remain viable over a period of years so that a return on the investment in asset creation will be fully realized, forecasting of future trends is essential. Then an organization can accommodate changes in a manner that will allow smooth evolution and modernization of assets over time. If knowledge acquisition is a craft, *technology forecasting* is an art. Short term forecasts of a few months can often be developed with reasonable confidence. Long term forecasts of several years are difficult to develop with confidence.

After the gathering of domain information by reverse engineering, knowledge acquisition, and forecasting, the information is integrated into domain models that can be used to support asset specification and development. This is usually done in an ad hoc manner because general methods do not adequately support comprehensive model synthesis of this nature. Domain models need to be validated in some way to establish confidence in their correctness and utility. Processes supporting model validation include walkthroughs, expert reviews, and trial application of assets derived from the models.

The goal of *Asset Implementation* is to produce the assets in the asset base. This could be done by creating the assets from scratch with guidance from the domain models as to what kinds of components should be developed. Alternately, a company may require that its software developers provide whatever code they develop to the software reuse librarians so that it can be considered for incorporation into the library. This latter case in which libraries acquire existing components is discussed in the next sections.

Figure 4.3–Decomposition of Reuse Engineering: The three main processes of engineering reusable assets, namely, creation, management, and utilization, are shown here with their many subprocesses.

- Asset Creation
  Domain Analysis and Modeling
  Domain Architecture Development
  Asset Implementation

- Asset Management
  Library Operation
  Library Data Modeling
  Library Usage Support
  Asset Brokering
  Asset Acquisition
  Asset Acceptance
  Asset Cataloging
  Asset Certification

- Asset Utilization
  Asset Criteria Determination
  Asset Identification
  Asset Selection
  Asset Tailoring
  Asset Integration

Asset Management

The Asset Management processes fall into two general classes: processes that focus on acquiring, installing, and evaluating individual assets in a library, and processes that focus on developing and operating libraries that house collections of assets, provide access to those assets, and support their utilization (see Figure 4.4 Managing Engineering). Asset Management overlaps in some ways with Reuse Management. Organizational assets, such as plans, are generally treated as part of the reuse infrastructure, while library support technology is generally considered the province of Asset Management. Asset Management addresses the selection and support of technology that is inherently asset-, library-, or domain-specific, or tailored to be so

Figure 4.4–Managing Engineering: The reuse cycle is shown with detail provided for the Management phase in which Library and Asset processes occur.

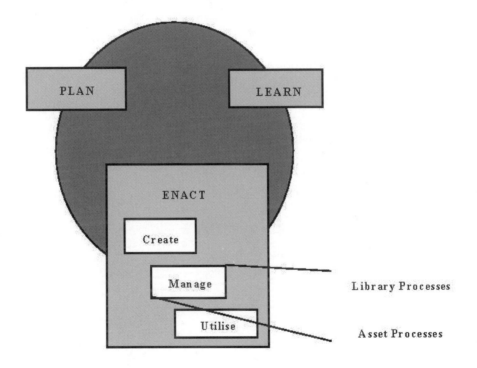

Library Processes

A library houses managed asset collections. A library need not be automated to effectively manage a collection of assets and serve a useful mediator role between Asset Creation and Asset Utilization processes.

The goal of *Library Operation processes* is to ensure the availability and accessibility of the library and its associated assets for Asset Utilization. This can involve a variety of activities, such as:

- Administration and operation of the physical library facility,
- Library access control and security,
- Periodic archiving and backup of library contents, and
- Support for interoperation with other libraries.

These activities are strictly operational in nature, and organizations may consider them to be aspects of general infrastructure. However, there are aspects of these activities that relate specifically to asset libraries and merit attention from an Asset Management perspective. Some typical library user roles, corresponding to some of the Asset Management and Asset Utilization processes, include library data modeler, asset cataloger, asset certifier, library operator, asset utilizer, and asset broker.

The goal of *Library Data Modeling processes* is to develop a data model for describing assets within a library. This library data model synthesizes the domain models, asset models, and assets. The specific approach is thus dependent on the characteristics of the Asset Creation products and on the objectives of the library in supporting Asset Utilization. If the library's objectives are to provide a basic search and retrieval capability for individual assets, it should suffice for the library data model to include mainly taxonomic information derived from one or more domain models. If the objectives are more ambitious, then the library data model must integrate additional elements of the domain models.

In addition to incorporating information produced by Asset Creation processes, the library data model also codifies information that specifically addresses Asset Management needs. For example, a model could include data elements to record asset certification information and user feedback data. In addition to simply operating a library and making assets available within it, Asset Management should provide a set of library services that anticipate and address specific asset utilizer needs. Examples of these kinds of services include:

- the collection and generation of asset data in a number of different formats, including a variety of media (e.g.,, paper and on-line files) and data representations (e.g.,, text and executables), and
- the operation of electronic hot lines to accept and resolve user complaints.

Specific tools can support activities such as viewing assets, executing assets for evaluation, extracting sets of closely related assets, and so on.

An often critical form of *Library Usage Support* is direct, personal assistance to users. These consultation services can be likened to the role of the traditional librarian in conventional book libraries. Such services can be automated to some degree, but may be most effective when rendered in person. This person-to-person approach can effectively lower the technological barriers to reuse that typical library software presents to many users.

A related form of library user support services is asset subscription, which allows users that 'subscribe' to a particular asset to be informed of all changes to that asset as it evolves. The kinds of asset changes about which a user can be notified include identification or resolution of errors, changes in classification, development of new variations, and addition of new usage history data.

Asset Processes

Related to activities considered library processes are asset processes. These include asset brokering, asset acquisition, asset acceptance, asset cataloging, and asset certification (Boeing, 1993). Localized efforts may monitor asset flows, interactions, and feedback among Asset Creation, Management, and Utilization processes, and apply that knowledge to work proactively with all concerned parties to improve effectiveness in particular areas. Such activities can be viewed as Asset Brokering processes.

The principal goal of *Asset Acquisition* is to obtain assets from external sources to support Asset Utilization activities. Asset Acquisition obtains assets that appear to be good candidates for inclusion in an asset library. The goal of *Asset Acceptance* is to ensure that an asset that is a candidate for inclusion in a library satisfies relevant policy, legal, and domain-specific constraints. The purpose of library policy constraints is typically to ensure that assets in a library satisfy at least minimal criteria for quality and suitability for use in Asset Utilization activities. *Asset Cataloging* incorporates accepted assets into a library classifying, describing, and installing them. Asset certification goes beyond asset acceptance and puts the 'official seal of approval' on an asset after rigorous testing.

Other perspectives on asset processes exist. One view emphasizes actual software rather than software-related documents and tends to call assets by the name 'components'. In this view, the library receives from its customers and others, recommendations for components to add to the library. A file may be maintained for every *proposed component* (GTE, 1992a). This file would note for the component its description, availability, and rationale for its request. The librarians evaluate each proposal for a component to ensure that the proposer has, at least, one application in mind, to assess the cost-effectiveness of the component, and to identify other beneficial characteristics, such as wide applicability and low complexity.

The library *acquires* reusable components from numerous sources. There is no absolute need for the library to contain a physical copy of each component. A component would be incorporated by reference only, if it is:

- maintained and distributed by an outside organization or
- executable code.

When a component is *incorporated by reference*, the library should provide on-line instructions for obtaining the component and documentation for the component.

The fundamental criterion for acceptance of a component into the library is cost-effectiveness. The cost of obtaining and reusing the component must be less than the cost of developing the desired capability directly. One aspect of a component is the method by which it was produced. A component developed with sound methods by a recognized team of software developers has a greater likelihood of being easy to reuse than a component developed in some other way. No product, however, can be considered reusable if it lacks an understandable description of its capabilities and clear instructions on its use. If a reusable component is incorporated by reference, quality assessment information is still required. The folder for a component ready for accession contains considerable information. This information should include a user's manual, testing data, and quality assessment. Once the necessary supporting material, including the classification of the component is available, the librarians *assimilate* the component into the library and distribute information about its availability to the library users.

Asset Utilization

The goal of Asset Utilization is to construct new application products using previously developed assets. The outputs from Asset Utilization include:

- Software Systems and other application products that are constructed from assets,
- New assets for incorporation into the asset base, and
- Feedback concerning the library and its assets.

Asset Utilization generally involves determining a set of criteria to use in selecting assets for reuse, identifying suitable candidate assets in the context of those criteria, selecting and tailoring assets to meet the criteria, and integrating the tailored assets with the target application.
The reuser must tailor assets that have been selected for reuse so that they satisfy target system requirements. This tailoring generally comes in two forms, either or both of which may be applied to any given asset:

- *Anticipated Target* system needs lie within the range of variability anticipated for an asset during Asset Creation; the asset encapsulates the variability through some set of tailoring interfaces (such as parameters); these interfaces can be used to resolve the variability to meet target system needs.

- *Unanticipated Target* system needs lie outside the range of variability anticipated for an asset during Asset Creation (e.g.,, there is a need for new features where no variability was anticipated); the asset thus provides no relevant tailoring interfaces that can be applied and must be modified to address the unanticipated target system needs.

To perform *anticipated tailoring*, an engineer must understand the range of variability an asset may accommodate and how the asset's tailoring interfaces are used to select among the variations. This information should be included in the library in the form of 'reuse instructions' for the asset, which may be augmented by examples. In addition to parameterization, another technique that can be used for anticipated tailoring is hand modification of the asset in accordance with precise instructions. An asset that can be tailored in this manner is typically called a template.
Unanticipated tailoring is more of an ad hoc process in which the engineer assesses the asset's shortcomings relative to system needs and then employs whichever strategies are appropriate to tailor the asset to those needs. This often involves hand modification of the asset to add desired features or remove undesired features. Modifications may also be needed to address issues such as performance, environment compatibility, and safety, reliability, or other quality factors.

Figure 4.5–Reuse Costs: Initially the cost of the reuse program is very high, as the library of reusable items is built. Returns cannot start until the library is usable, and then will tend to be low, as the library needs to become suited to the developers who use it and gaps in the libraries content are filled. The final level of return is uncertain, it should become high and remain high, but this will depend on the quality of the reuse library, it's retrieval system and the willingness of developers to reuse.

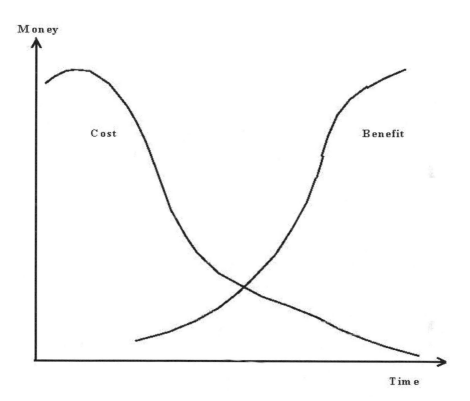

Costs versus Benefits

Software reuse is difficult for companies to initiate because it has the least desirable cost structure, initially very high, recouping over time. Start-up costs include setting up the software component library that will be

needed, training staff to set up the library, populating the library and training the software development teams to use the library software and reuse
the actual components. Gradual returns over the life of the library should
pay for initial costs over a period of time, and return profits, but may not.
There are other possible benefits in the quality of the software produced
and minimization of developer time and resources, but these benefits may
be difficult to measure (see Figure 4.5 Reuse Costs).

To be willing to provide an *investment in reuse*, companies will need
proof of the benefits of reuse. Some of the benefits of reuse are tangible,
for example the time to build a project should be reduced. But the way to
prove that project development time had been reduced would be to build
a project using conventional means and then to 'go back in time' to before
it was written and to create it again using exactly the same people, without the knowledge they gained by building the system in the first case,
with reusable components. This is of course impossible, and would in any
case be inconclusive since the benefits of reuse will vary from project to
project. Most of the benefits of reuse, increased quality of programs and
documentation, less testing required, fewer skills needed within the
development team, and the production of components available for future
projects, are difficult to measure.

Reuse is only *cost effective* if it actually takes place. If on a project
reuse options are investigated, i.e., requests for reusable components are
formulated and submitted to the library system, and some components
retrieved and investigated for suitability and none of them prove suitable
or none are found, then a perhaps significant amount of time has been
wasted by the developers. Also the library has failed to live up to its
expectations on this project and thus no money used to set up and run the
reuse library has been recouped. For a new library and reuse methodology unless very significant amounts of money have been spent creating the
library, then low returns on reuse should be expected on quite a regular
basis. The components created (since reusable ones could not be found)
should be used to add to the library, but this will be more expensive than
custom-creating the components for just this project.

The method used to estimate *reuse costs and benefits* should be compatible with the methods used by the rest of the company. The two quantities of primary importance are:

- the net saving to the individual user for each instance of reuse of a
  component and
- the net saving to the company from all reuses of the component.

The quantities in the analysis can be expressed either in some monetary unit or in labor hours. Benefits may be categorized as (GTE, 1992a):

- The savings due to reuse, S_R, is the sum of costs avoided each time the component is reused.
- The service life, L, is the useful lifetime of the component in years.
- Demand, is the number N, of times the component is likely to be used during its service life. If the costs and benefits may vary from year to year, then the demand should be apportioned per year as N y where y = 1, 2, ..., L.

The costs associated with a component may be formalized as:

- The cost to reuse, C_R, is the cost incurred each time the component is reused, including retrieval and tailoring costs.
- The accession time, T_A, is the amount of time between the decision to acquire the component and its availability in the library.
- The accession cost, C_A, is the cost to add the component to the library.
- The maintenance cost, C_M, is the cost to maintain the component in the library. Again if yearly costs vary, the maintenance cost distribution C_{My} where y=1, 2, ..., L is the cost to maintain the component for each year of its service life.

Risks which might be incurred need to be estimated. These may be due to a dependency on a particular environment or configuration, obsolescence of the design or code, and legal obstacles. These risks can be accommodated in the preceding variables as appropriate.

The *net saving* NSR to the individual for each instance of reuse is the difference between the saving due to avoided cost and the cost to reuse, or in symbols, $NSR = S_R - C_R$. The total savings from all instances of reuse is NSR multiplied by the number of reuses. Thus the net savings from all reuses NSP is the total saving minus the accession and maintenance costs, or in symbols, $NSP = (NSR \times N) - (C_A + C_M)$.

The NSP may be calculated on an annual basis. For each year, $NSP_y = (NSR \times N_y) - C_{My}$. This calculation assumes that the accession cost is incurred prior to the beginning of the first year of service and is recorded separately. The cost estimation method may include an adjustment for the fact that future cash flows decrease in value with time at a rate that can be given the discount rate i. Thus the annual discounted NSP can be given as $DNSP_y = ((NSR \times N_y) - C_{My}) / (1 + i)^y$.

To compare two potential reusable components to determine which to acquire for the library and which not, the cumulative discounted cash flow CDCF for each would be determined and the component would be preferred with the higher CDCF. $CDCF = DNSP_1 + DNSP_2 + ... + DNSP_L - C_A$. With the appropriate data and these formulas, a company can better plan its reuse investments.

Depending on the management strategy adopted by the software development company, the costs of reuse may be absorbed by the developer in the hope of creating similar projects later, and thus recouping the investment that way. Or alternatively the developer may form a partnership with the client, where initial startup costs and any later benefits are both shared.

Legal Issues

If the client of a software house is willing to allow the software house to reuse components developed for them for other clients who need similar systems, then the software house has more reasons to practice software reuse. However who it is that is the *owner* of a component developed for a project could be a thorny issue. Does permission need to be sought to include a component developed for a project in a library, if that component is generic? Should commission be paid to the instigating client? These issues may be soluble by written agreements listing terms and conditions between the client and the developers.

Legal issues affect a reuse effort as they effect any other endeavor that involves the utilization of the work of others in the creation of new work. There must be clear legal boundaries defining what is reuse and what would constitute plagiarism. *Copyright* exists in most western countries to some extent, and motion pictures and books have well defined protection in law (Lahore and Dworkin, 1984). In nearly all countries legal protection of software is more hazy as the law attempts to get to grips with and catch up with the technologies to hand.

Within the European Union moves are under way to standardize legislation between the various member states. Computer software is generally regarded as intellectual property and as such may be protected under patent and copyright law. The *copyright* protects the expression of the software, the routines and the order in which they are called. Whereas *patent* protects the industrial realization of the concept. That the rationale behind the software is protected by patent extends the protection beyond simply the code to cover flow charts or pseudo code and thus protects the author against language translation, reverse engineering and adaptation of the code. Although under the United Kingdom Patents Act 1977 computer programs as such are described as expressly non-patentable inventions, patents may be granted for new and improved products incorporating inventive concepts embodied in a computer program (Edwards, *et al*, 1990).

The granting of a patent to an individual or organization grants to the holder monopoly rights over the subject of the patent for a period of normally twenty years. The criteria upon which a patent application will be granted are that it is of a technical nature, is new and makes a technical contribution to the known art. Taking out a patent offers greater protection to the author than is available under copyright as there is no onus to prove copying has taken place. The major drawback is the time taken to process patent applications and that making the application for a patent reveals to the public the nature of the invention.

Copyright of software is a property right and means literally the right to copy the literary or artistic work produced by the author. Literary content may refer to the program code or documentation. Artistic work may refer to the user interface generated by the software. *Copyright* more importantly restrains others from reproducing or adapting the contents of an original work. Copyright protection is offered automatically - by order of law - on the recording in writing (or storage in an electronic format) of a copyright message stating 'Copyright 1994 Our Company'. This applies copyright to an original work and protects against copying and adaptation of the work. The existence of a copyright, however, does not prevent another organization arriving at a similar solution providing it does so by independent means. In this respect a copyright, unlike a patent, does not offer monopoly rights over a product. The copyright is applicable for a period of fifty years from the date of publication.

For software reuse libraries bought from a vendor, the vendor's licensing agreement will generally include clauses amounting to non-exclusive licensing of the software. As they are sold as reusable components, they may be incorporated into a product which may be either for distribution within the company or to be sold as a commercial product.

Impact

To successfully set up a reuse program involves transferring research approaches to reuse into standard industrial practices. Four main stages are identifiable in the transfer process:

- the Audit,
- the Planning Stage,
- the Implementation, and
- the Evaluation.

The audit involves examining the current system and investigating options for retaining parts of the existing process. This stage is especially important because for reuse to succeed, it is, of course, important to build on any existing reuse practices, and in any case, it is common sense to determine the current state of affairs before attempting to change it. In any case, a baseline is required to determine whether or not the change has been successfully accomplished. Moreover, at the start, it is essential to determine the most fruitful areas in an organization where people are likely to *champion reuse*, or where the most benefits from reuse practices are likely to accrue.

Once an *audit* has been completed, the reuse planning team should be in a position to plan a course of action with the aim of creating a situation where reuse is standard practice. In formulating the reuse program plan in the areas where existing reuse has been identified the aim should be to improve on existing practice if possible, for example with better support.

In planning for implementation, some general consideration of the channels of communication within an organization may be helpful. During the actual *implementation stage*, it is helpful to build on any successes in acceptance of reuse. Strategies to achieve this include encouragement of reuse champions and communication of best practice. As with any new practice, it is better to implement a small but successful program gaining the confidence of staff and then build it up, rather than attempting to establish a more grandiose scheme and lose the goodwill of staff. In all accounts of successful reuse, the importance of ensuring that there is management support for the reuse program has been stressed.

In considering the factors that influence effective reuse, attention must be given to the process of reuse, supporting technology, potential objects of reuse, standards, and other technical aspects. While technical issues do require attention, it has been increasingly recognized that consideration must be primarily given to non-technical factors such as management, scope of reuse program, economics and, perhaps most important, the social implications. In this context, the use of *quality circles* has been reported as offering an opportunity to introduce the concept of reuse within a company as part of a broader concern to improve overall quality of the enterprise.

One of the main obstacles to software reuse in the large is the understandable tendency of software producers to protect their intellectual property against competitors to maintain a commercial advantage. The collaboration of these commercial entities to extend the benefits of software reuse across company boundaries requires the existence of a *benevolent organization* to co-ordinate and fund the reuse activities. In the United States this role is played by federal bodies, such as the National Aeronautics and Space Administration and the Department of Energy, who actively encourage software reuse by making available to contracted organizations reusable components produced on behalf of the federal body to all contractors in an attempt to reduce development time for software as a whole. The initial cost for the federal body in creating the reusable components is thus offset by the benefits incurred as the components are reused in later projects.

Epilogue

The themes about reuse as expressed in the *Conceptual Framework for Reuse Processes* are:

- Software reuse has both management and engineering dimensions,
- Reuse should be applied as a 'first principle'. That is, reusable product should always be considered as the basis for work before creating new products.
- Learning and managed change, based on measurement history, and innovation, are essential to reuse.
- Technical, organizational, and educational infrastructure is essential to reuse, and must be designed and managed to support it.
- The asset producer, broker, and consumer roles are important, separable aspects of reuse that form distinctive patterns of activity within the Reuse Engineering idiom.

The Framework is generic with respect to domains and technologies. It can be applied in an organization of any size, at any organizational level. It provides a basis for the analysis of reuse processes and the definition of reusable assets.

The individual reuse processes gain synergistic value when viewed as modular building blocks that can be used to construct a wide variety of reuse-specific process configurations reflecting different planning levels, organizational structures, and interaction patterns. To support the construction of process configurations, the Framework should include a set of composition techniques to connect the processes together in a variety of ways. These techniques provide a flexible and scalable composition approach enabling the Framework to capture aspects of reuse-based engineering practice not easily described with traditional software life cycle models.

Modifying the software life-cycle for reuse involves everyone involved in the creation of software. Formulas exist for determining the costs and benefits but obtaining realistic values for the variables in the formula is challenging. Everyone from developers to those who manage budgets and plan projects and even the final customers for the programs produced will play some role in the ultimate value of the reuse effort. If reuse is successful at a company, then everyone involved will benefit. Developers will not have to waste time developing software repetitively and costs will be reduced in the long term. These *savings* can be passed to the customer in reduced costs, faster delivery, and increased reliability.

Chapter 5
Standards

The key to reuse is that people agree on constructs and methods. Standards reflect this. Very few *standards* specific to software reuse have been widely accepted by the international community. However, numerous organization-specific reuse standards have been developed and they are reviewed in this chapter.

The *Reuse Planning Group* was created by the IEEE Software Engineering Standards Committee in April 1995 with the following assignment:

> The Reuse Planning Group will define for SESC a statement of direction for IEEE standards related to the analysis, design, implementation, validation, verification, documentation, and maintenance of reusable software assets as well as their supporting infrastructure in the creation of new applications.

The group began with an analysis of the needs of various users of standards. Then a list of available, normative documents on the subject of software reuse was compiled. These documents were evaluated for the role that they might play in the standardization process. Finally, the document articulated a model relationship between principles and practice that new reuse standards should satisfy (Baldo *et al*, 1997). Using these frameworks, it made recommendations.

The Master Plan for Software Engineering Standards (SESC, 1993) provides a list of user *expectations for standards*. In overview, users expect that the standards will ensure that software will provide a correct, standard solution for well-known problems. The software will perform as specified and expected, and is user friendly. The software can be modified within pre-defined limits which will meet specific requirements without difficulty. The software satisfies operational, functional, and performance requirements. The software is verifiable. The software quality and cost can benefit from the reuse of artifacts (requirements, design, test cases, and code). The software has sufficient associated data available to make an intelligent acquisition choice. Use of standards should promote reusable and portable software process artifacts and should permit reuse of development environments. It should be possible to accurately estimate the time and budget for software maintenance work. Standards should include criteria for certification of software as fit for use and reuse.

Expectations

User expectations have been annotated to categorize the kind of standard that might address such an expectation. The lists of expectations here are based on those contained in the IEEE SESC *Master Plan for Software Engineering Standards.* At the beginning is a list of postulated roles that reuse standards might fill. Each expectation is annotated with one or more roles indicating that standards fulfilling the annotated role should address the expectation.

The postulated *roles* are:

<<dom>>   Standards describing domain analysis methods or other methods for identifying reuse opportunities could address these expectations.

<<prod>> Standards describing the production of reusable software assets could address these expectations.

<<doc>>   Standards regarding the documentation of reusable software assets could address these expectations.

<<lib>>   Standards for libraries of reusable assets could address these expectations.

<<cert>>   Standards for certification of reusable assets could address these expectations.

<<int>>   Standards regarding the mechanisms or frameworks for integrating reusable assets could address these expectations.

<<swlc>> Standards addressing how software reuse is integrated into the overall software life cycle and/or life cycle processes could address these expectations.

<<adopt>> Standards regarding the adoption of reuse practices (including economics) could address these expectations.

<<NA>> These expectations are regarded as not applicable, usually because software reuse seems to introduce no issues beyond those faced in other forms of software development.

The software user expects standards to ensure that:

- Software is categorized in a useful manner. <<lib>>
- Software will provide a correct, standard solution for well-known problems. <<dom>><<cert>><<prod>>
- Software will be measurable, measured, and sufficient for the intended application. <<NA>>
- Software is supported, maintained, and has a planned enhancement cycle. <<swlc>>
- Software purchasers expect standards that ensure that:
- Processes, including selection criteria, for evaluating and selecting purchased software. <<swlc>><<cert>>
- Information on the software package describes form, fit and function of the software. <<dom>><<lib>><<cert>>
- The required environment for software is specified so that incremental capability that is needed is easily identifiable. <<dom>><<lib>>
- For each software release, there is a clear, concise articulation of differences, features, new functions, limitations, and constraints. <<doc>><<lib>>

Software asset managers expect the standards to provide requirements or guidelines that ensure:

- Criteria for determining the value of software as an asset will be available. <<adopt>>
- Cost models for modifying versus replacing software are reliable. <<adopt>><<dom>><<swlc>>

- Identification of reuse benefits of existing software assets. <<adopt>><<swlc>>
- Common methods for identification and labeling components and media to facilitate software library organization. <<lib>>

The lists of expectations can be regrouped by role. For instance, the software asset manager expects the standards to provide requirements or guidelines that ensure that the theory for software depreciation schedules has a practical business foundation and that cost models for modifying versus replacing software are reliable.

Existing Related Standards

Which existing documents might be of use in a standardization program? Documents are considered that are *normative*, (i.e., standard-like, in nature). Each document is described in terms of its purpose, scope, and audience. An evaluation is performed to assign each document a candidate usage.

Evaluation Criteria

The purpose of evaluating existing documents is to determine how they might appropriately contribute to standardization efforts regarding software reuse. Evaluation criteria are formulated to support the making of such recommendations. The result of each evaluation will be an assignment of a *candidate usage* for the document. There are four categories of usage called base document, normative advice, helpful information, and not useful with the following descriptions:

- Suitable for use as a *base document* in a standardization effort.
- Good, *normative advice* that could contribute to a standardization effort.
- *Helpful information* that could be used whenever appropriate.
- *Not useful* for standardization efforts.

In determining the candidate usage, the following characteristics are considered: Relevance, Impact, Normative Nature, Currency, and Quality.

Relevance is determined on the basis of:

- significance to software reuse of the issues treated by the document and
- the extent of the document's potential for dealing with user expectations.

The *Impact* criterion evaluates the extent to which the document has already achieved acceptance in the reuse and software engineering community. Impact is determined on the basis of the following characteristics:

- How broad was the community of consensus involved in writing the document?
- How broad is the current community that is applying the document?
- How effective has the document been in improving software reuse practice?

The Normative Nature criterion evaluates the extent to which the document provides normative direction rather than information. Three ratings are provided:

1. *Conformance:* To achieve this rating the document must have a statement of conformance. Furthermore, it must be possible to evaluate conformance in a manner that is reasonably objective, (e.g., by measurement or by an administrative law judge).
2. *Guidance:* The document provides advice and recommendations.
3. *Information:* The document provides only information.

The *Currency* criterion evaluates the extent to which the document is suitable for application today and in the foreseeable future. Three ratings are provided: Far Seeing, Current, and Obsolescent, with the obvious interpretations of each. Finally, the quality criterion depends on the clarity and accuracy of the document.

Evaluation of Existing Documents

Next, existing documents are briefly described in terms of their audience, purpose, and scope. The descriptions of the document are grouped by the organizations that issued or maintain them.

Software Engineering Standards Committee (SESC)

One of the major contributors of software standards is the *IEEE Software Engineering Standards Committee* (SESC). Most of the products of the SESC that are related to reuse are submitted to it by the Reuse Library Interoperability Group (RIG). The RIG is an independent group of reuse library users, operators, and vendors that are developing specifications for the interoperation of reuse libraries. The RIG is comprised of more than 150 individual members and about 20 organizational members participating at various levels of activity. The RIG's work is progressed to the status of standards via its Memorandum of Understanding with the IEEE SESC.

The RIG has produced a Data Model for Reuse *Library Interoperability* - Basic Interoperability Data Model (BIDM) to describe the minimal information that reuse libraries should be prepared to exchange in describing their assets. This document is already an IEEE Standard. The RIG has also developed extensions to the BIDM that may be used for explaining the manner in which assets were certified for quality or other attributes and guidance for performing certification. This document is being processed as an IEEE Standard. The RIG is in a very early draft phase of a standard for the binding of the BIDM (IEEE Std 1420.1) to HTML and to SGML.

ARPA

The United States *Advanced Research Projects Agency* (ARPA) has several programs of worth to RIG. Its Conceptual Framework for Reuse Processes (Boeing *et al*, 1993) was described in the previous chapter. The primary audience is project planners, process engineers, and reuse advocates. The principal purpose is to define a conceptual framework that describes reuse in terms of the processes involved. The framework is intended to be generic with respect to domains, organizations, economic sectors, methodologies, and technologies. The scope of the CFRP is limited to identifying the processes involved in reuse and describing at a high level how those processes operate and interact. In so doing, it indicates how some reuse processes can be integrated with other processes. It does not prescribe how reuse can be implemented. Legal, business, and acquisition aspects of reuse are outside the scope. The CFRP is considered a highly relevant document with high impact (see Figure 5.1 ARPA Evaluation).

Figure 5.1–ARPA Evaluation: The document titles are in the first column. The document attributes are given in the first row. The other entries are the values on each attribute for each document.

Document	Relevance	Impact	Nature	Currency	Quality	Usage
CFRP	High	High	Guidance	Far Seeing	Good High	to Base Document
Strategy	High	Some	Conform	Far Seeing	Good	Normative Advice
Direction-Level	Relevant	Some	Guidance	Current	Good	Normative Advice

The *Reuse Strategy Model* (Boeing, 1993) has an intended audience of business and project planners whose organizations are making the transition to domain-specific, reuse-based development practices. The document is intended as a planning aid for reuse-based projects. It provides a set of dimensions for characterizing current reuse practice and a suggested process performing the characterization. Based on the results, a variety of reasonable goals are provided. The model presumes that the project has been characterized with respect to the STARS CFRP, and that the organization wishes to move toward domain-specific, reuse-based development practices.

The *Direction-Level Handbook for Reusable Defense Software* (Paramax, 1992) is directed toward Department of Defense acquisition executives to facilitate their institutionalization of software reuse. The document provides a framework to assist acquisition executives in establishing plans to manage reuse across the systems under their purview. It is intended to assist in initial planning for new acquisitions as well as other critical points within the life cycle.

United States Department of Defense

The United States Department of Defense *Software Reuse Initiative* has produced several documents of interest to the standards community. The Software Reuse Executive Primer (DoD, 1995) targets defense acquisition managers. It provides a simple and understandable overview of software reuse. The primer appears to be applicable within the defense acquisition community and specific to their particular problems and procedures. This Department of Defense document has had little impact (see Figure 5.2 DoD Document Evaluations).

Figure 5.2–DoD Document Evaluations: Two DoD documents are listed in the leftmost column and their attributes are named in the top row.

Document	Relevance	Impact	Normative Nature	Currency	Quality	Candidate Usage
Primer	Relevant	Some to Little	Information	Current	Good	Helpful Information
Business Model	High	Some	Guidance	Far Seeing	Good	Normative Advice

The *Software Reuse Business Model* (DoD, 1995) targets management involved with incorporating reuse into the acquisition process and individuals responsible for making reuse happen. The document is far-seeing and should be of normative value in future reuse standardization. This document presents a business model detailing the incorporation of reuse principles into the acquisition cycle of software systems within the Department of Defense. The focus is the steps involved in performing systematic software reuse including activities, information, processes, and tools.

United States Armed Forces

The United States Armed Forces have produced various software reuse standards. In the *Guidelines for Successful Acquisition and Management of Software Intensive Systems* (USAF, 1995) software reuse is a central theme. The audience is anyone responsible for the acquisition, management, or support of major software development efforts. The document is rather focused on Department of Defense systems and, thus, not of normative value for international standardization.

Figure 5.3–Armed Forces Standards: The two Armed Forces documents are listed in the leftmost column and their attribute values in the interior cells of the array.

Document	Relevance	Impact	Normative Nature	Currency	Quality	Candidate Usage
Acquisition	Relevant	Some	Information	Current	Good	Helpful Information
Guidelines	Relevant	Some	Guidance	Obsolete	Good	Helpful Information

The document *Software Reuse Guidelines* (USAF, 1990) provides guidelines for U.S. Army development groups undertaking software reuse. Management and technical issues are discussed. Management issues include: impediments to reuse; the creation of incentives for reuse; and incorporating reuse into a software development and maintenance process. Technical issues include: domain analysis; preparing reusable assets; assuring asset quality; and classifying, storing, and retrieving assets. Some sections place emphasis on Ada. This and the other Armed Forces document are of moderate value to further reuse standardization (see Figure 5.3 Armed Forces Standards).

Software Productivity Consortium

The *Software Productivity Consortium* has produced several documents. *The Reuse Adoption Guidebook* (Virginia, 1992) targets business organizations that want to begin adopting software reuse practices to better meet their goals or to become more competitive. It is more specifically oriented to those that need to further examine the applicability of reuse technology and need support in identifying and implementing required changes. The *Guidebook* describes a reuse adoption process controlled by the organization's objectives, opportunities, and current capability. An important component is a reuse capability model that assists in understanding current capabilities and establishing goals.

The Reuse Adoption Guidebook model is strongly tied to the Software Productivity Consortium Synthesis framework. Synthesis provides a domain engineering process to create a product family and an application engineering process to create specific instances of the family in response to customer needs. Nevertheless, the document is highly relevant and provides normative standards material.

The *Domain Engineering Guidebook* (Software Productivity Consortium, 1992) is intended for use by business-area managers, project managers, and engineers. The guidebook defines two instances of the Synthesis approach for the development of families of software products. Again this document is considered highly relevant.

Others

The American Institute of Aeronautics and Astronautics has a *Guide for Reusable Software: Assessment Criteria for Aerospace Applications*. The *Guide* is intended for use by software personnel, including managers, engineers, librarians, analysts, and researchers. The Guide is intended to focus on the domain of aerospace applications, but much of the advice is generally applicable. The section on domain analysis surveys various approaches and then develops criteria for domain analysis and the principal products of the analysis. The next section describes asset assessment criteria in three categories: domain (suitability to application); reuse (potential value of assets to other projects); and software (development of reusable components). The final section discusses how assessment information can be captured in a library and suggests some criteria for evaluating reuse libraries. The document is a candidate for normative advice.

The National Institute of Standards and Technology has prepared a managerial overview of software reuse (Wong, 1986). The report provides an overview of the various aspects, problems, and benefits of software reuse, including both management and technical issues. The Reuse Planning Group assessed that the report was of little impact and obsolete currency. A similar document from the same institute (Wong, 1988) received a similar negative assessment. A glossary of software reuse terms from the National Institutes of Standards and Technology (Katz, 1994) was judged as of little use because the audience is intended to be only the Department of Defense software reuse community.

Bell Canada has produced software process models that are relevant to reuse. One process capability model called *Trillium* targets customers who acquire software-intensive systems (Bell, 1994). Trillium is a process maturity assessment method, comparable to the Software Engineering Institute's Capability Maturity Model. One of 28 road maps focuses on software reuse. The evaluation shows the document to have high impact, high relevance, to be far-seeing, and to be a candidate as a base document for a reuse standard.

Recommendations

The *Master Plan* of the IEEE SESC describes an evolutionary approach to reorganizing the collection of SESC standards. Future SESC standards related to reuse can be positioned within this master plan. The master plan provides a four-layer model structured as follows (see Figure 5.4 Organization of SESC):

1. Terminology
2. Master Road Map
3. Program Elements
4. Technique Standards

Figure 5.4-Organization of SESC: The four major components are shown in their order

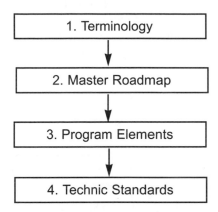

The top layer, Terminology, is provided principally by IEEE Glossary of Software Engineering Terminology. Terms specific to software reuse will be adopted via the mechanism of including them in the glossary.

The second layer, *Master Road Map*, is intended to be an overview document describing the relationships among key SESC standard as well as with those of other organizations. In general terms, software reuse will find a place in that description. The bottom layer, Technique Standards, consists of standards describing techniques which are at a detailed level or which might be applied in a number of different contexts.

The third layer, *Program Elements*, is the key one for positioning reuse standards within the SESC collection. SESC has four program elements:

3.A Customer - relationships with the customer of a project.

3.B Resource - resources that can be used by a project.

3.C Process - processes that can be followed by a project.

3.D Product - products that can be produced by a project.

Each program element can be viewed as a stack of three components:

3.x.1 Policy or Principle Standards

3.x.2 Element Standards

3.x.3 Application Guides

The *Policy Standards* provide objectives for the various standards collected within the program element. The Element Standards are high-level standards providing normative guidance on important software engineering activities. The Application Guides provide advice on how to apply the Element Standards within particular situations.

Reuse standards might occupy the following position in the Master Plan:

- 3.B.2 Resource Element Standards, e.g., reuse libraries and their interoperation. The existing Reuse Interoperability Group standards fit here.
- 3.C.2 Process Element Standards, e.g., reuse process adoption, reuse capability assessment, domain analysis processes and adaptation of software life cycle processes to reuse
- 4. Technique Standards, e.g., coding guidelines for reusable components, documentation of reusable components

In the remainder of this section, candidate standards will be labeled with their anticipated positioning within SESC's Master Plan. Finally, a few alternatives that were considered, but rejected, will be described briefly.

Potential New Standards

There is sparse evidence regarding the effectiveness of specific reuse techniques. The principal drivers and obstacles to successful reuse are non-technical in nature. Even though the requirement for reuse is contemporary, much of the technology is still emerging. These observations argue for a *conservative approach*, standardizing only what is necessary to permit the continued evolution of the field. Those necessary items might include a framework for the discussion of reuse processes and practices, terminology, acquirer/supplier provisions, and library interfaces.

The SESC collection should articulate principles for software reuse. These principles should be traceable to a set of fundamental principles of software engineering and based upon successful *patterns of usage* (see Figure 5.5 Principles and Patterns). This would ensure that the standards are both principled and based on actual practice.

Patterns of usage are important as reflected in these four recommended further types of standards for reuse:

- a set of reuse *processes* (or reuse-motivated modifications to normal life cycle processes) that are traceable to the principles.
- a set of *practices* that implement the processes.
- an *assessment mechanism* for the processes and practices.
- implemented processes, practices and assessment mechanisms together regarded as *patterns* of usage.

Figure 5.5–Principles and Standards: Software principles lead to reuse principles which lead to patterns of use.

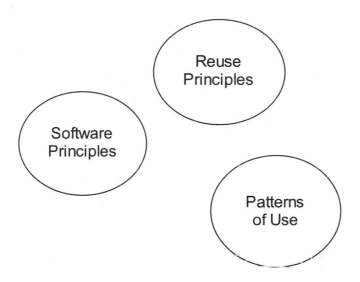

A standard for *principles of reuse* would provide a vocabulary and a framework of principles to organize and rationalize other standards related to software reuse. It would include a glossary of terms for software reuse and principles for software reuse

A list of candidate principles for this document follows:

- Build a software domain architecture as a framework for reuse activities.
- Use a software development process that promotes and controls reuse.

- Reuse more than just code.
- Practice domain engineering.
- Integrate reuse into project management, quality management and software engineering activity.
- Organize the enterprise to facilitate partnering to achieve reuse across product boundaries.

Even though technology for performing domain analysis is immature, there is great demand for it. Some successful analyses have been performed and there is a body of work explaining how such analysis should be performed. The purpose of a *domain analysis standard* would be to describe the minimum required processes and products of domain analysis.

Most software reuse processes are not distinct from the normal life cycle but instead must be integrated into other life cycle processes. Some acquirers are demanding software reuse even though the effectiveness is not quantitatively proven. Fortunately, some successful reuse efforts have occurred and there is a body of work describing these efforts. These considerations argue for a *process standard* that explains how software reuse processes may be incorporated into the life cycle. This might be a supplement to ISO and US 12207 explaining how reuse processes are incorporated into the life cycle processes of 12207. Relevant base documents would be:

- ISO 12207 and
- STARS CFRP

Other Normative Advice would come from:

- ANSI J-016
- CARDS Direction Level Handbook
- DoD Software Reuse Institute Reuse Business Model
- Software Productivity Consortium Reuse Adoption Guidebook

No reuse practice or assessment specifications are recommended for standardization. None of the specific *practices* have proved sufficiently repeatable to merit standardization. Those wishing to apply software reuse techniques should select practices consistent with the principles and processes described in higher level standards.

Even though technology for software reuse is immature, some acquirers are demanding that it be performed and desire to understand the capability of potential suppliers for adopting reuse practices. This sort of *capability assessment* should not be performed in isolation but in the context of the more general capabilities of the supplier. A supplement to SPICE is recommended that explain how reuse processes may be assessed within the context of the life cycle processes of 12207.

Rejected Alternatives

The topic of *assessing reusable components* might be regarded as among the most desirable of standards, but it cannot be pursued as a standard at this time because of a lack of available art in this area. Groups of vendors might be able to agree on conventions for their products that restrict them in such a way as to permit assessment. Work by consortia in this area might be useful. The state of the art in this area should be reevaluated periodically.

Configuration management (CM) is a particularly interesting issue because the CM desired for a reuse library is fundamentally different than the CM used in a software development program. During software development, the raison d'etre of CM is to make sure that the latest, best and most bug-free version of a component is the one that gets integrated into the final product. On the other hand, the reason for CM in a reuse library is to make sure that the appropriate version of the component is made available to a user. (For example, a user might choose to reject an "improved" version of flight control software if the improvement was done for purpose of prototyping and was never flight-rated.) So, CM in software development has the goal of controlling the user's choice of components while CM in a reuse library has the goal of informing the user of the detailed relationships between components that are similar but slightly different. Frankly, this new role is poorly understood. It presents some technological challenges to extend CM out of controlled environments while still maintaining control. For example, components must be given names that last "forever," that remain unchanged when the component is moved to a new library, and that permit the users to satisfy themselves that the component has not been altered—even by the original author. It is one of the items in the area of "library organization and operation" that is technological immature and lacks proven effectiveness.

The Reuse Planning Group also evaluated and rejected several other topics as *not suitable for standardization* at this stage. Reuse adoption guidance has little evidence of repeatable effectiveness and little evidence of de facto consensus. Reuse development practices are too specific to particular tools and technologies and too low-level and voluminous. Library organization and operation have no measures of effectiveness.

Conclusion

In 1992 the *North Atlantic Treaty Organization* (NATO) issued three documents about software reuse as standards for NATO. When one reads the NATO documents, one appreciates that they are NATO-specific. In other words, they are plans for how NATO itself will conduct software reuse activities.

The observation about the NATO-specific standards is merely one example of a more general phenomenon in reuse standardization—the most tangible reuse standards are *specific to a single organization*. That's because successful reuse practices touch many parts of an organization's methods and culture for doing business.

To better appreciate the organization-specific character of the most tangible reuse guidelines consider an example. Assume a standard says that any reusable subroutine must be documented with its "intended function." In an organization indoctrinated in Harlan Mills's structured programming techniques, this has a precise mathematical definition that is well understood because of the corporate culture of pursuing Mills's techniques (Mills *et al*, 1986). If one generalizes this standard to other organizations and expects them to use the Mills's techniques, one would be faced with the complaint that "this organization documents its software differently." So in an effort to be general one would relax the standard to a requirement that software be documented—a very non-specific requirement that can be satisfied in a variety of superficial ways. In broadening the applicability of the standard, one robs the standard of its ability to discriminate. This phenomenon appears over and over again in software reuse standards.

Standards can be developed by many different kinds of organizations (Rada and Berg,1995). IBM and Motorola have developed corporate standards for reuse among their employees. Government agencies have developed standards for how government contractors must follow software reuse processes. Relatively little has been done explicitly about software reuse by official *standards development organizations*.

The major international standards organization relative to information technology is ISO-IEC JTC1. The standards from the US Military and NATO, are not JTC1 standards. JTC1 has one project underway that is particularly germane to software reuse. This is the "Software Process Improvement Capability dEtermination" (SPICE) project.

SPICE provides road maps for important software practices. Reuse is one of the practices covered by SPICE. SPICE is designed to provide software organizations with an internationally recognized mechanism to support their continuous process improvement programs, and to help managers ensure that the process is aligned with the business needs of the organization. SPICE will also help purchasers determine the capability of software suppliers and identify risks.

The IEEE SESC chartered a *Reuse Planning Group* to develop a plan. That plan recommends four new efforts:

- a standard describing principles of software reuse—principles that individual organizations could satisfy in a variety of ways;

- a standard describing the characteristics of domain analysis— domain analysis though little understood is now frequently practiced;

- a supplement to the ISO 12207 life cycle process standard (Moore and Rada, 1996) to describe how reuse practices relate to the 12207 processes; and

- a method for performing capability assessment for suppliers of reusable components, probably within the context of SPICE.

The recommendations are notable also for the efforts that were considered but *rejected*. For example, the group rejected efforts for standards related to "reuse development practices" because they were regarded as being too specific to tools and technologies and being too low-level and voluminous. Standards for library organization and operation were rejected because reliable measures of effectiveness do not yet exist. Guides for reuse adoption were rejected because there is little evidence of repeatable effectiveness and because there is little evidence of de facto consensus. Perhaps most notably, an effort to write a standard for the assessment of reusable components was rejected because of the concerns regarding the ability to "scale" reuse practices beyond the scope of a single organization.

The US Department of Defense is already writing software development contracts that require reuse. Yet, *no internationally recognized standard* for how software reuse should occur exists. Such standards are needed.

Two *kinds of standards* are being developed. One kind is technical and focuses on the software assets that are to be reused. Another kind is social and guides the human side of software reuse. The artifacts are much less complex than the people. Developing a suite of standards that apply seamlessly to the people and their artifacts will not be easy.

Section 3
Organize, Retrieve, and Reorganize

In this Section three phases of reuse engineering are examined. These phases are the initial organization of a library of reusable components or concepts for later reuse, the retrieval of relevant components from the library, and the reorganizing of these components to form a useful system. In other words, this life cycle includes:

1. Representation of software items that can be reused, i.e., semantic and syntactic means or conventions for describing them - *Organization,*

2. Later retrieval of these items by another developer - *Retrieval,* and

3. Development of software using reusable components - *Reorganization.*

Document and object oriented approaches to all three phases are discussed and compared, as are applications of both techniques to program code, and higher levels of abstraction such as software requirements. The discussion of program document retrieval is augmented by practical examples.

A major problem to be overcome in the deployment of software reuse techniques is to identify appropriate methods for the *classification and retrieval* of software items. If retrieval is not made easy for developers, they will prefer to re-write the component from scratch. At the same time classification must be simple and cost effective to justify the cost of setting up and maintaining the library of items against the cost of developing the items each time from scratch. These twin aims of simple classification and powerful retrieval are contradictory in themselves, as will be explained.

Chapter 6
Organizing

In constructing, or maintaining a reuse system, an early step is to build a repository of reusable concepts and components for developers to use as a resource. These components can come from many *sources* (see Figure 6.1 Component Sources). These components need to be processed to ensure that consistency and quality are maintained throughout the library.

Organizing refers to collecting, analyzing, indexing and storing information so that it can be easily accessed later. Before software documents (here documents being any information produced during the software life-cycle, such as a piece of code or a requirements document) can be successfully reused, they must be somehow organized (Rada, 1991). Documents that are to be reused should be organized into a carefully designed system that reflects their topic. There are several methods for organizing items. At one extreme each document is stored in a file and an index associates strings with the files that contain them, while at the other extreme a knowledge base replaces the documents entirely, representing them in its structure.

Indexing

After material has been collected and analyzed (as described earlier), it should be indexed. The two most important basic approaches to document indexing are the interpretive and structural approaches. With *interpretive indexing* the document is read and understood before index terms are assigned (Kaplan and Maarek, 1990). In contrast, the structural approach uses the frequency of word usage in natural text as an indicator of relevance of the contents to a topic without semantic interpretation

being assigned to any word. In the interpretive approach 'indexing concepts' are chosen to represent a document expressed in a natural language
such as English (see Figure 6.2 Keyword Approach). The indexers may
have complete freedom of choice over what they can use as an indexing
term to represent a concept, or they may have guidelines to follow over
how certain concepts should be represented. This approach without
guidelines is quick to implement, but can lead to inconsistent indexing
terms for documents in the library, especially if the library is large, and
has many people indexing components for it.

Figure 6.1–Component Sources: Components may arrive for the library from a
software house, or from public domain sources, or from projects on-going which
have developed new components suitable for reuse.

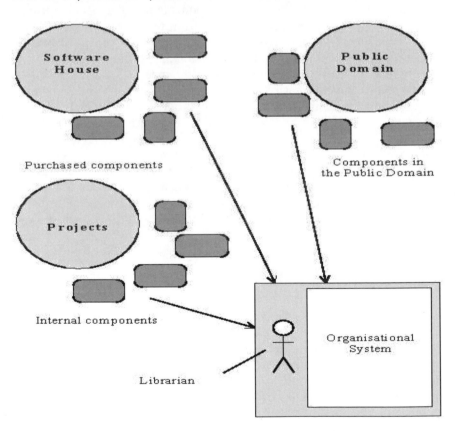

Structural indexing is based on the observation that writers usually repeat certain words as they advance or vary their arguments, or elaborate on an aspect of a subject. This approach has motivated a number of automatic indexing algorithms for information retrieval systems (Yu and Salton, 1997) An important automatic indexing approach is frequency based. A typical word frequency indexing algorithm is to:

1. Identify all the unique words in the document set.
2. Remove all common function words included in a stop list (such as 'a,' 'the,' 'or,' 'and,' 'is,' ..., etc.)
3. Remove some suffixes and combine identical forms of the same word (stems). This reduces a variety of different forms such as 'constructs,' 'constructing,' 'constructor,' and 'constructed,' to a common word stem 'construct.'
4. Calculate the frequency of occurrence of the resulting word stems.
5. Assign a mid-range of frequencies for terms to be considered for indexing.
6. All terms that are within the mid-range are then selected as indexing terms.

Frequency-based indexing generates a flat description, i.e., a frequency ordered set of unrelated index terms for each document. A more sophisticated indexing mechanism can identify the relationships between the co-occurring index terms.

Figure 6.2–Keyword Approach: A list of concepts to index this paragraph.

"Computer Aided Instruction (CAI) systems have improved greatly over the years. Their knowledge content is still however low, and the system decisions, though usually correct cannot be analyzed for the reasoning behind them. Knowledge can be stored in the domain of a learner model in a variety of ways, and thus a student may have to acquire knowledge using several different methods."

Possible indexing concepts:

> Computer Aided Instruction,
> knowledge content,
> learner model.

Document Outlines

Successful interpretive indexing requires understanding a document's content. A document's outline may provide a valuable guide to this understanding. Most well prepared documents have an outline. The *outline* manifests itself in the layout of the document as highlighted and numbered headings in the document body, as well as in a separate listing at the beginning of the document in the 'table of contents.' This physical layout helps people understand the logical structures of the document and find thematically-organized sections in the document. This means that there is an existing organization of themes (or sort of domain model) in the document that can be easily observed and perhaps utilized in organizing the document for reuse systems. Analysis of the outline provides a quick and simple insight into the content of the document. Tools can automatically extract an outline from a document and thus split documents into themed sections, showing the relations between these sections (see Figure 6.3 Outline Analysis).

Obviously the size, balance and depth of this structure varies from document to document. There are no strict rules for the construction of headings or outlines, though some patterns in headings do exist. In many cases, headings are noun phrases, such as 'Introduction to Database System Concepts,' 'Physical Data Organization' and 'Protecting the Database Against Misuse.' But headings may even be complete sentences, such as 'What Makes Interlisp Unique?.' The heading of a section should briefly describe the contents of that section, and headings can be seen as 'content index' terms for a document. It follows therefore that one may extract index terms from the headings to represent more generically the sections under those headings. For example, both 'The Network Model' and 'The Relational Model' may be indexed by the key word 'Model.'

In many documents, some subheadings *inherit* attributes from their parent heading. For example, the heading 'Hardware' under 'Site Requirement' means 'the site requirement on hardware.' This dependence may continue on several levels. In some scientific documents, headings repeat. Documents of a given type, such as requirements documents, may all have the same outline. Some company policies require such conformity of outlines. Furthermore, the documents of a given software life-cycle fall themselves within a kind of high-level outline whose headings may show some relationship across documents (see Figure 6.4 Relations among Outlines). When one studies the nature of the relationship between headings in an outline one observes three kinds of relations, structural, hierarchical and attributive (Mili *et al*, 1996).

- The *structure relation* refers to parts of a document outline which are not fundamental to the major topic of the document but serve rhetorical or record-keeping functions. For example the title of the document connects to the 'Introduction' heading via a structure relation, and the 'Date of Creation' heading has the same link from the title.

- The *hierarchical relation* includes the traditional partitive (a part of) and inheritance (kind of) relations. For instance, the link from 'Function' to 'Subfunction1' would be of the hierarchical type.

- The *attributive relation* is a non-hierarchical relation. For instance, if the section headed 'Function' includes subheadings 'Inputs' and 'Outputs,' then the relation from 'Function' to these subheadings would be attributive.

Figure 6.3–Outline Analysis: By analyzing the hierarchy of the outline of a book it may be possible to automatically break the book into domains.

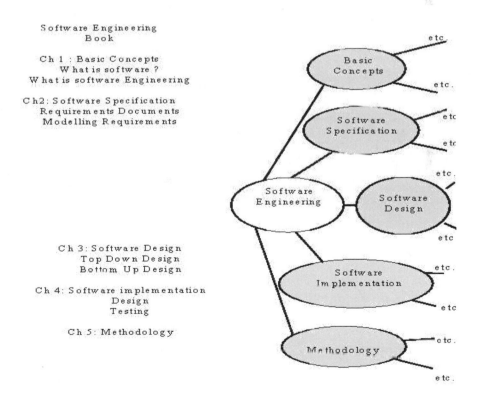

Such a characterization of outline relations can greatly facilitate the manipulation of outlines. These outlines are not, however, as frequently used in supporting reuse as they might. Some outlines are not sufficiently well organized or descriptive to guide reuse, so additional effort is needed to abstract the contents of these documents and to represent that information in easily maniputable ways.

Figure 6.4–Relations among Outlines: Each box represents a document of the software life-cycle whose title is indicated in its upper left corner. The arrows show how a heading of a document in one phase of the software life-cycle can be related to a heading in another document of the same software life-cycle.

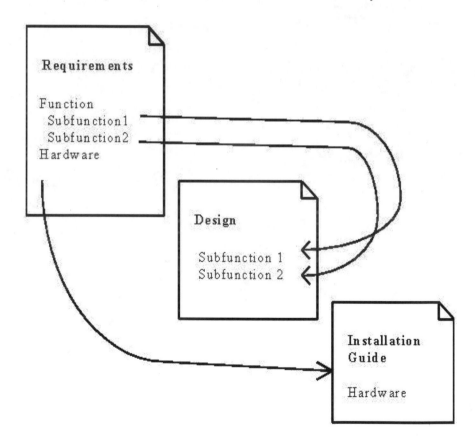

Domain Models

A high-level organization of an information space may be reflected in a model of that space. Given that the information space addresses a particular topic or domain, the model could be called a topic model or a domain model. A domain model should identify the objects and operations on those objects that are common to an application domain. Also important are relationships and constraints between the objects and their corresponding properties or attributes, that are likely to be used by developers in the process of searching for reusable components - these must be made explicit. One part of a domain model may be a classification. A classification groups together like things. An enumerated classification scheme (Ranganathan, 1937) assumes a universe of knowledge divided into successively narrower classes that include all possible classes (see Figure 6.5 Enumerated Example). These are then arranged to display their hierarchical relationships. An example of this scheme is the Dewey Decimal system.

Thesauri

The enumerated classification has little flexibility, as it is usually represented as simply a strict hierarchy of terms with no further attributes and no term occurs in more than one place in the hierarchy. A thesaurus extends the enumerated classification by allowing a few other attributes for each terms, in addition to the attribute of hierarchical location. A thesaurus may be presented in a hierarchical, 'Table of Contents' form or as an alphabetical sorting. It includes preferred terms (descriptors) for indexing, and non-preferred terms as lead-in terms (or synonyms) to corresponding preferred terms. The preferred term essentially labels a concept. Two basic relationships between concepts are hierarchical (broader than, narrower than) and associative relations. Several other attributes for a thesaurus term can be defined, including dates of entry (see Figure 6.6 Thesaurus Terms Table).

A thesaurus supports organizing and finding documents in both object- and document-oriented systems (though in itself it is object-oriented). With a thesaurus one document can be indexed under several terms. A user can broaden or restrict the results of his or her search by asking the system to refer to the thesaurus. Thus the thesaurus provides the retrieval system with some natural language 'ability.'

Figure 6.5–Enumerated Example: In this greatly simplified classification scheme of the sciences, an enumerated classification scheme has been imposed. For many cases this is perfectly adequate. However, if the topic 'Biological Paradigms for Computer Vision' had to be classified the system fails, since this topic is equally relevant at A and B in the above classification.

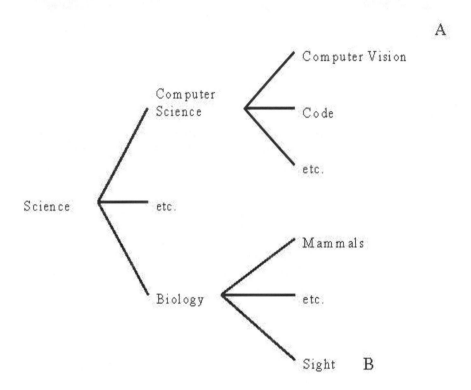

Thesauri are normally part of a larger system and are best built with regard to their function in that system. It is possible to build a thesaurus first and then use it to index the documents to be added to the library. This is described as a top-down approach. To do this requires an amount of prior knowledge of what the library is likely to contain. Alternatively, in the bottom-up approach the documents may be indexed using free terms and then the thesaurus is constructed after accumulating a number of these free terms. Consistency must be maintained in the terms used and their structure as preferred and non-preferred terms. When the function required of the thesaurus is retrieval, as it largely is in the software reuse world, the best method for building the thesaurus is a mixture of these. The drawback of using thesauri is the effort needed to build and maintain them.

Figure 6.6–Thesaurus Terms Table: This shows the terms associated with the preferred term 'Snakes.' Top terms represent main classes in a classification system, in this case the main class being 'Animals.' It is also possible to define a relationship between prior designations for a concept and its current naming, in this case 'Serpents' as an older naming for the concept of 'Snakes.' In software documents this is useful for version following.

Attribute	Value
Preferred Term	Snakes
Definition	
Date of Entry	June 3 1992
Top Term	Animals
Broader Term	Reptiles
Narrower Term	Rattlesnakes
Associated Terms	Worms
Synonym	Vipers
Prior Term	Serpents

Faceted Classification

A thesaurus basically provides a hierarchy of concepts with little other information about each concept than its hierarchical position. To extend the thesaurus, one may expand the representation of each concept in it. A faceted classification is a kind of extended thesaurus. Faceted schemes are easier to expand than enumerative schemes. They are more flexible, more precise, and better suited for large, continuously expanding collections. A software component may be described by a set of {facet, facet term} pairs:

- A *facet* is a fixed set of concepts from which to view components.
- A *facet term* comes from the library's list of representative terms for the particular facet.
- Any number of pairs may be applied to a given software component.

Typically a domain will have about ten facets.

A typical set of *software facets* might include:

- object: a software engineering abstraction operated upon by the software component,
- function: an action performed by the component, such as sort or delete,
- algorithm: any special method associated with a function or method, such as "algorithm, bubble" associated with "function, sort" ,
- component type: the particular kind of software life-cycle product, such as code or design,
- language: the language used to construct the component, such as Ada, C, or English, and
- environment: any hardware or software for which the component is specialized, such as Unix.

A component is described by assigning appropriate facet terms for all applicable facets.

A description for a sort routine might use the facet 'object' twice but the facet 'environment' not at all (see Figure 6.7 Descriptions of Sort Routines). In a more flexible sort routine, the facet 'object' has disappeared, since the object to be sorted is a generic parameter of any type. This example also illustrates that more than one facet term may be given for a single facet. Thus the user who has an application-oriented view might be served equally well as the user who has a software-oriented view, if the librarian has put both an application-oriented facet term into the facet and a software-oriented facet term into the same facet.

Figure 6.7–Descriptions of Sort Routines: The facets for two different software components, called Rigid Component and Flexible Component, are given. Note that the 'Flexible Component' does not use the facet 'object.'

Facet	Facet Term	
Name	Rigid Component	Flexible Component
object	address	
object	mail code	
function	sort	sort
algorithm	binary sort	binary sort
component type	code	code
language	Ada	Ada

Code Organization

Reuse of code, usually in very informal ways, is almost as old as programming itself. All *high-level programming languages* are in themselves a kind of code reuse system. They provide a method of manipulating the hardware at quite a high-level which reuses large amounts of very low-level code in each instruction. Some aspects of operating systems offer a similar function. Libraries of functions in high-level languages continue this abstraction a level higher. Systems like the UNIX pipe function (which is described later in this book) extend this abstraction to include reuse of whole programs typically themselves written in a high-level language using sub-routines. Newer languages, such as object-oriented languages like C++, and generic functions and packages in ADA, provide powerful facilities for the programmer to make abstractions.

Figure 6.8–Component Code: A sample piece of code to show how keywords can be considered to exist in ordinary code.

```
PACKAGE int_queue ( parameters ... )
--        --Description--
--        AUTHOR: D. Chaplin
--        DATE: 28th May 1992
--        NAME: int_queue
--        COMPANY: NKM_Software
--        VERSION: 4.2
--        FUNCTION:   A variable size queue for
--           integers.queue is a first-in-
--           first-out (or FIFO)
--           data structure.
--
--        --Classification--
--        CATEGORIES:         Data Storage,
--                            Abstract Data Type.
--
--        KEYWORDS:           queue,
--                            first-in-first-out,
--                            data storage.
--
--        --Storage Requirements--
--        MEMORY ALLOCATION:        as needed.
--
--        --Dependencies--
--        LIBRARIES:                needs math.lib.
--
-- *** Definitions ***

. . . .
end int_queue;
```

Code that is to be reused can vary in size from a small block of code, of say a dozen lines, that performs some minor function, to a procedure of thousands of lines that performs a complex operation. There are problems and advantages to reusing both sizes of object. Smaller components are less productive since their functionality is not as great due to their size, but are easier to combine and modify to achieve a different goal from that originally intended, since they encapsulate a single function.

Functions can, however, be expected to receive and return their parameters differently, both in number, format and type. Using small functions means that these 'structure clashes' will occur more frequently, since there will be a greater number of individual routines.

Keyword-based approaches to indexing programs are similar to those used for documents, namely that an indexer uses a natural language, such as English to describe the content of a component. Indexing terms could be added to the start of an actual program code component (see Figure 6.8 Component Code).

A form of *outline-extraction* may be possible for a well-commented program. The comments might include headings in a way analogous to the headings in a conventional document. However for many programs, their existing comments are not written to this standard. It should be possible to add comments to the code to achieve this, although this would be time consuming and therefore remove many of the advantages of using this method.

Object-oriented software is widely seen as a possible major contributing factor in the wider acceptance of software for reuse (and was briefly discussed in the chapter on the software life cycle). This is due to features of object-oriented languages such as data encapsulation and information hiding, which reduce or eliminate much of the effort involved in making components suitable for reuse. In recent years several object-oriented languages have appeared, for example Smalltalk 80, together with object-oriented extensions to some existing functional languages, such as Object Pascal, Objective C and C++.

Object-oriented programs are made up of interacting components called objects. These *objects* may correspond to real world entities i.e., bank accounts, or to computer hardware and software components. Others may correspond to data structures such as lists, stacks, and queues. Software construction using object oriented languages is the assembly of objects to form a system. Each object is by its nature well defined since it implements a real world 'object' and its scope is fixed and defined by a real world entity. Object-oriented programming encourages programmers to assemble complex programs from simpler components.

With object-oriented document classification schemes, domain modeling is important, this is also true in object-oriented program component schemes. Program components are described in a subject-oriented hierarchy depending on the functions offered in the program component. The *domain model* can be refined to several levels of granularity, at the finest level this should lead to subclasses that contain program segments which are different versions of the same program segment or functionally equivalent program segments.

Frameworks

One extension to the object-oriented methodology is sometimes described as frames or frameworks. Of course, the term framework has many meanings in the world at large and may be used in generic ways in software engineering also. However, for the purposes of software reuse, a *framework* is defined as a reusable, semi-complete application that can be specialized to produce custom applications (Fayad and Schmidt, 1997). In contrast to earlier object-oriented reuse techniques based on class libraries, frameworks are targeted for particular business units or application domains.

A framework enhances extensibility by providing explicit hood methods that allow applications to extend its *stable interfaces*. Hook methods systematically decouple the stable interfaces and behaviors of an application domain from the variations required by instantiation of an application in a particular context. The run-time architecture of a framework is characterized by an inversion of control. This architecture enables canonical application processing steps to be customized by event handler objects that are invoked via the framework's reactive dispatching mechanism. The framework's dispatcher reacts by invoking hook methods on pre-registered handler objects, which perform application-specific processing on the events. The framework determines which set of application-specific methods to invoke—this is the inversion of control.

Developers in certain domains have been using frameworks for many years. *The Microsoft Foundation Classes* is a contemporary graphical-user interface framework that has become the *de facto* industry standard for creating graphical applications on personal computer platforms. For numerous complex domains, off-the-shelf frameworks do not exist, but the developers in those domains have each developed their own frameworks. Java is spreading new frameworks like AWT and Beans.

Frameworks are a component in the sense that vendors sell them as products. But frameworks are more customizable than most components, and have more complex interfaces. Classes in the object-oriented sense have not realized much success in general as reuse devices. Frameworks are harder to learn than individual components or classes. However, a good framework lends itself more to reuse.

Frameworks provide a reusable context for components. A framework provides a standard way for components to handle errors, to exchange data, and to invoke operations on each other. The so called *component systems* such as OLE, OpenDoc, and Java Beans, are really frameworks that solve standard problems that arise in building compound documents and other composite objects. Frameworks provide the standard interfaces that enable existing components to be reused (Johnson, 1997).

Frequently, the two views of framework reuse, referred to as whitebox and black-box approaches to reuse, are simultaneously present in one framework. Features likely to be common to most applications can be offered and therefore reused as black boxes with minor changes. On the other hand, the class library accompanying the framework usually provides base classes or *white boxes* that can be specialized by adding subclasses as needed and that are easily integrated with the rest of the framework (Brugali *et al*, 1997).

Patterns and frameworks are similar. Both are efforts to extend the object-oriented approach so that it incorporates domain analysis and addresses particular problem areas with partial solutions of a larger granularity than would be otherwise addressed by traditional objects or classes. While each pattern describes a decision point in the development of an application, groups of related patterns can be organized as a tree or graph in which each pattern leads to a series of other patterns. Such a structure is called a pattern language and represents the sequence of decisions leading to a complete design, so a pattern language becomes a method that guides the development process. This complements general development methods by adding domain-specific, concrete advice to their general guidelines. A pattern language supports the development of the framework that in turn supports the use of the patterns.

Books are now available that present patters or frameworks for particular domains. For instance one book focuses on *business patterns* (Fowler, 1997). Two broad types of patterns are described within the book: analysis and support patterns. The analysis patterns are groups of concepts that represent a common construction in business modeling. They may be relevant to one or more domains. Support patterns are patterns in themselves. Their role within this book is to show how the analysis patterns may be applied. The patterns within this book include accountability, observations and measurement, referring to objects, inventory and accounting, and planning and trading. The support patterns include layer architecture for information systems.

Epilogue

The way in which software information is organized in a library is crucial. It constrains how the developer may use the library. Techniques for the organization of components may be document-oriented or object-oriented.

The document-oriented approach relies on the extant structure of documents and on free-word indexing. A document-oriented system is easy to set up and offers many methods for organizing documents fully or, at least partially, automatically. But document-oriented methods are weak in many retrieval situations, since the information they provide about the structure of documents and the structure into which documents are organized is quite simple. Only basic retrieval methods, such as searching for topics explicitly mentioned in a document, is possible. Automatically extracted information is usually a subset of the information stored in the document, and thus offers less information about the documents than the documents themselves and only weak associations between them. This can be improved by human indexers reading the documents and assigning keywords to describe the contents of the document, but it is hard for this indexing to be kept consistent over large databases of thousands of documents, or with several indexers working simultaneously. This causes many problems at the retrieval stage, which are described in the following chapter.

Object-oriented systems basically depend on some form of high-level abstraction or model, commonly called a domain model. Object-oriented techniques are labor-intensive for the set-up stage. However a rich structure is produced that can be interrogated in many ways and provides many advantages to a searcher. A thesaurus provides a system with some basic knowledge of a domain, thus allowing 'intelligent' searches which find documents using terms related to desired terms rather than simply failing. The emphasis can be on making retrieval easier, at a cost of making organization more complex, time-consuming and expensive. Or the opposite, where it is retrieval that requires expertise and may prove unproductive, but organization is simple.

Chapter 7
Retrieving

Before a developer can write a program using reusable components, the components to be reused must be obtained. A reuse library will not be used effectively, if it is not relatively easy for its users to retrieve the desired information from it. Users must be allowed to be flexible in how they *search* for information. If the library is searched with a specification or partial specification of the required component, then the system should be able to determine how much of that specification can be met by copying and combining existing items from the library, in an ideal case at least. In a situation where the library does not contain the desired information on a particular topic, the user should be able to browse for and examine any possibly related components in the library (see Figure 7.1 Flexible Searching).

Retrieval Specification

As described earlier, the software life-cycle can be viewed as a refinement process, which starts with the developer having only very informal and abstract specifications of what the final product should look like. Unfortunately it may be important to know in the early stages of this process which reusable components are applicable, since existing reusable items can only be integrated, if the system is designed to accommodate the reusable items. However, at these early stages, the user of the library might have difficulty expressing what precisely is required. Despite the vagueness of the retrieval specification, the resulting search of the library should lead to helpful information. The developer should be able to progressively modify the query as retrieved items add to their mental model of the library contents. This can be called iterative searching or browsing (see Figure 7.2 Iterative Searching).

Figure 7.1–Flexible Searching: In this system 3 avenues of exploration are available to the developer, he or she can pose a query as a 'Full Specification' of the component, part of that specification a 'Partial Specification,' or by 'Browsing' through the components that exist in the library.

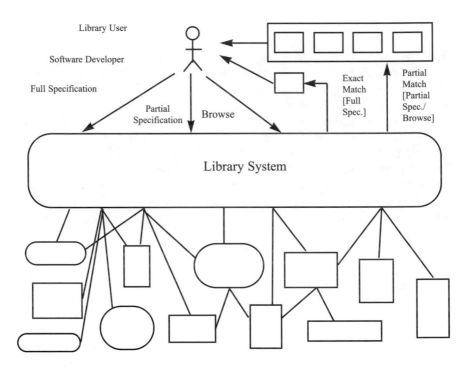

Figure 7.2–Iterative Searching: This is a description of a technique in which the user poses an initial query to the library retrieval system and uses the results returned by this query to formulate a new and more detailed query. This is then used to query the system, and this process can then be repeated.

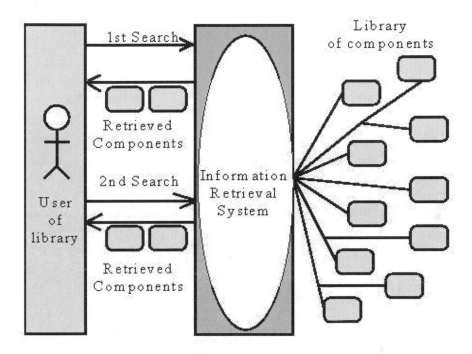

With a thesaurus-indexed collection, if the user asks for document components about for example 'depth-first traversal,' and if the system has no document components indexed with that term, then the system might find the term closest to 'depth-first traversal' in the thesaurus and perform retrieval on that term. For instance, if in the thesaurus 'graph algorithms' is a broader concept than 'depth-first traversal,' and if the retrieval system has document components indexed under 'graph algorithms,' then the system should return those document components to the user (see Figure 7.3 Guaranteed Return). Thesaurus-aided searching may need to be complex (Mili, 1991). A developer may need, for example, a multiplication routine. Multiplication can be performed (as it often is in very low level languages) as a series of shifts and additions. Normally shifting and multiplication would not be synonymous, and thus a component on shifting would not usually be offered to someone who searched for multiplication. This is a simple example and in this case many developers could make the link themselves and submit searches for shifting and addition components themselves. However in the general case it would be hoped that retrieval systems would be able to decompose a search in that way. From even these simple examples it can be seen that the demands upon the retrieval mechanism to be used for software reuse are many and varied.

Figure 7.3–Guaranteed Return: The user has requested text on 'depth-first,' and the thesaurus has been followed to find related text.

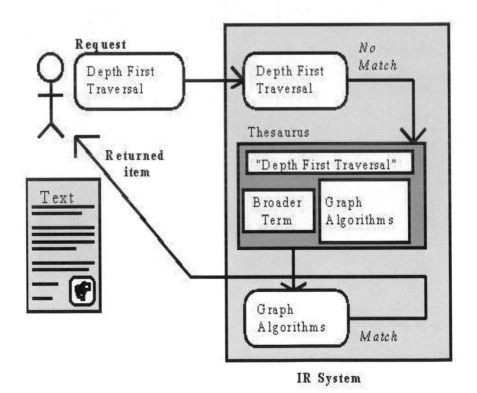

IR System

Document Retrieval

Document-oriented retrieval approaches include searching for key terms expressed in a natural language, such as English. When a large library containing many thousands of items is indexed by more than one person the terms adopted can become inconsistent. This *inconsistency of terms* chosen to represent components can lead to different keywords being used to represent the same concept in two components. Problems may also exist in searching the library for very common phrases like 'system' that may have been used as an indexing term for very many unrelated items. Efforts can be made to help this situation if careful controls over the indexing terms are exercised.

The keyword form of Information Retrieval is widely used in Japanese software houses, where reuse of software components is an integrated activity in software development. The stored components are indexed manually using keywords covering the technical or application-oriented aspects of the component. The tools applied for retrieval are very simple (Matsumoto, 1987). Much of the success enjoyed using this informal method is due in part to many specific Japanese social and working conditions, rather than their implementation of this method. The *Japanese* use training procedures encouraging software reuse and standardized methods for software description and development, in addition most Japanese software houses enjoy only very small staff turnover with the result that informal contacts with fellow employees allows useful components to be found without relying solely on the retrieval system.

Free-text retrieval requires that the user knows, or is able to determine what free-text term would represent the document for which he or she looking. This approach will fail to find documents which are relevant but use a different term, such as 'sorting' and 'ranking' (unless good thesaurus support is given, which due to the effort required to maintain thesauri, in some ways defeats the advantages given by using this method).

If the system is using the concept model described in the previous Chapter, then techniques for finding documents can use the attribute values stored for each of the components. These attributes and their values carry more information about a document than a simple list of keywords. They give not only an indication of what subjects a document is discussing, but how those subjects are relevant to a topic (see Figure 7.4 Concept Model Links). This kind of linking among concept models is especially important in situations where hundreds of documents are available and many thousands of links are possible.

A retrieval system should not produce a bewildering selection of topics from which to choose at any point in the process of traversing a thesaurus or hierarchy of classes. The number of sub-classes from which the user is to choose at any point should be limited to an acceptably small number, ideally about twelve. The thesaurus can be further exploited to aid the user in searching. Starting at the root node of the thesaurus, the library system may ask the user a question, defined by the indexer, about their desired document. From this the system can determine which branch to follow from that node. By repeating this process the system can traverse the thesaurus and find the desired concept under user guidance (Saurel, 1985). To apply this method requires a well structured and understood domain, like mathematical applications, for which a comprehensive set of questions can be defined to guide the system, and for a human indexer to take the time to create all the questions, and to ensure that if the addition of new concepts requires a restructuring of the thesaurus that the questions are still valid in relation to the new structure.

Program Retrieval

Several methods for the retrieval of software documents have been discussed above. Next methods that can be used to retrieve existing code are outlined. Some of these approaches are similar to those for retrieving ordinary documents, but there are specific constraints to take into account when retrieving program code.

The simplest technique for specifying a search is by using a small piece of code that the developer would expect to find in the target routine, such as an Ada statement or a list of commands that are expected to be in the program. This is in many ways analogous to *full-text searching* for code. The string may need to be exactly specified or in a more sophisticated system wildcards may be allowed, for example printf(*%f*) may find all programs that contain the command printf with a floating point number regardless of the other parameters used in each case. This searching method makes it difficult for the library to find related components without some automatic way of generalizing from such a precise definition. It is more useful, particularly in the early stages of the software development life-cycle, to use a less specific representation, one which can describe a component in terms of what it needs to be able to do rather than how it could be able to do it.

Figure 7.4–Concept Model Links: This diagram shows three concept models. A plain text system would link all three with equal weighting. The links can be seen to be accurate as there is a logical 'chain' of topics from 'Archivers' to 'Dynamic Interfaces.' Although compression is significant to the 'MPEG II' Model, it is a sub-issue of dealing with motion video. In the 'Archivers' Model it is central. Similarly the 'MPEG II' document though relevant, is not as relevant to 'Dynamic Interfaces' as a document about 'Novel Interaction' would be. This difference in emphasis is important.

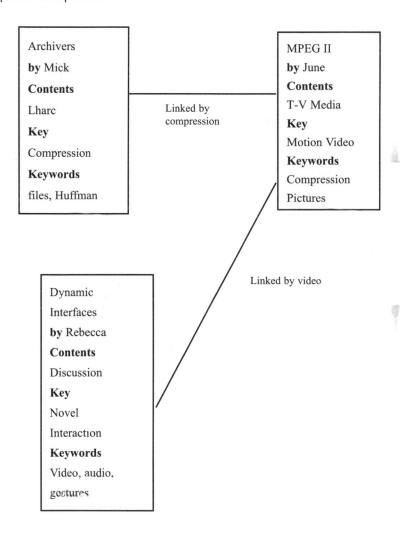

Formal methods for specifying the *semantics* of a software item include the Z-Schema or the Vienna Development Method. Unfortunately there are many varying methods, none of which is especially prevalent or standardized, therefore a library could not be designed to support all of them, or any particular one without restricting developers. Also specifying a component in terms of its semantics can be a time consuming and tedious task, and still requires a very good idea of the function of the component. But, a specification of this form is in a language independent form, and thus can be used to search a library which contains components in more than one programming language using a single retrieval system, even though of course a user of the library will only very rarely be in a position to be able to use a component regardless of its language.

With programs, domain analysis should ultimately lead to sub-classes that contain programs which are different versions of functionally equivalent programs. Even with well defined sub-classes which would often be hard to achieve in practice there can be problems comparing the programs in a sub-class. Two dummy package headers for an abstract data type will be used for an example (see Figure 7.5 Package Headers). These two packages in an Ada-type pseudo language define some abstract storage mechanism called a 'box' and allow some operations to be performed on that 'box' to move 'item's from box to box. The two packages are similar but not the same. One package does not offer a 'MOVE' command, to move an 'item' from one 'box' to another. However the two *packages* are functionally equivalent since the user may simulate a 'MOVE' by performing a 'COPY' on the 'item' to be moved and then 'DELETE' on the original 'item.' A search by a library user for an abstract data type of this kind should retrieve both of these items. In larger and more complex programs the commonality between two routines or packages may be considerably more subtle.

There is a minimal model of the data types that can be defined for both routines (see Figure 7.6 Second ADT). This model outlines a specification for all items in this sub-class of components. The user of the library then searches with a minimal model specification and the library retrieval system matches it with the stored model for that sub-class. This is sometimes called the 'Family Interface' method (Parnas, 1979) since the minimal model provides a common interface to all the programs in a component subclass or 'family.' However the user of the library has to be able to define a minimum model of the desired component.

Figure 7.5–Package Headers: Two basically functionally equivalent, but differently specified components.

```
package an_ADT is

        -- Available types are.
        type box is private;
        type item is private;

        -- Available functions are.
        procedure MOVE(item, box, box);
        -- Move an item from one box to another.
        procedure COPY(item, box, box);
        -- Copy an item from one box to another.
        procedure DELETE(item, box);
        -- Delete an item from a box.
        procedure CLEAR(item, box);
        -- Clear an item in a box.

end an_ADT;

(2)
package another_ADT is

        -- Available types are.
        type box is private;
        type item is private;

        -- Available functions are.
        procedure COPY(item, box, box);
        -- Copy an item from one box to another.
        procedure DELETE(item, box);
        -- Delete an item from a box.
        procedure CLEAR(item, box);
        -- Clear an item in a box.

end another_ADT;
```

Figure 7.6–Second ADT: This specifies the minimum or family interface for the two components.

```
        package generic type ADT is
        type box is private;
        type item is private;
        procedure COPY (item, box, box);
        procedure DELETE (item, box);
        procedure CLEAR (item, box);
        end another_ADT;
```

Retrieval systems may utilize 'grammatical' slots for software (Oh *et al*, 1994). One example of these 'grammatical' slots for software includes (Batory *et al*, 1993):

- Actions (what the component does) for example Sorting;
- Nominals (what the component does it to) for example Linked Lists;
- Modifier (any particular way in which it does what it does) for example Bubble or Exchange (sorting).

An indexed software component is found by describing its characteristics according to these slots. For example a string searching routine might be found by the user entering the modifier term 'find,' the nominal 'string' and action 'search.' A database of this kind can be supported by a thesaurus of all the possible terms that can be used in a slot. A grammar specifies how the terms may be used in combination, to avoid nonsensical searches. These systems are useful in that they are structured but do not require that the user specify queries in a complex formal language.

Retrieval Systems

Many software document retrieval systems exist in the form of on-line help systems. These systems typically lack a faceted classification or domain model but do illustrate powerful features of document-oriented systems. The UNIX and Andrew help systems are next described in terms of their retrieval support.

UNIX man Command

Every major command on a UNIX system has an associated man page which describes its function (Kernighan and Pike, 1984). These entries vary in size between one and several pages and are all stored in a standard format to make retrieval of specific information from a document easy (see Figure 7.7 Sample Man Page). Users may retrieve these 'man' pages in many ways depending on how man is invoked at the command line:

- Print or display the one-line description accompanying a set of manual entries specified by a keyword. For example, man -k initialization lists all one-line manual entries relevant to 'initial-ization.'

- Print or display the one-line description accompanying a specific command specified by name. For example, man -f lp gives all the one-line manual entries relevant to the 'lp' command.

- Print or display the whole manual page specified by name. For example, man cat gives the manual page or pages for 'cat.'

Figure 7.7–Sample Man Page: This shows a generic description of a typical UNIX man page.

name_of_prog(1) name_of_prog(1) NAME

name_of_prog - one line description of how the program works.

SYNOPSIS name_of_prog [-option1 -option2] **DESCRIPTION**

More detailed textual description of the program and its options and how these options affect the use of the program.

OPTIONS

-option1 describes the effect of this option -option2 describes the effect of this option etc.

EXTERNAL INFLUENCES

How other programs, and global environment variables affect the operation of this program.

EXAMPLES

(of use of the program) To do such a thing use :

name_of_prog -option2

WARNINGS

List of known problems or bugs with the software.

FILES

What ancillary files are needed to run the software, or are used or expected by the software.

SEE ALSO

Related programs which also have man pages, these are typically the programs which affect the 'External Influences'

Any term mentioned in the main title of a help file of a utility can be used as a search term. There is also an option to search for a keyword in a specific section of the man page, for example to search for printer settings in the 'External Influences' section.

This is a very useful system for *experienced users*, but not for beginners or people who are looking for a new command, since it demands that the user knows quite specifically what they are looking for before they can find it. If the on-line help does not contain an entry on a particular topic, then the user is simply informed there is no manual entry corresponding to that topic, and no help is given to enable the user to find a related or equivalent program held in the system.

The Andrew Help System

The Andrew help system is part of the Andrew Toolkit (Zanger, 1996). The *Andrew Toolkit* provides a total environment for the integration of diagrams, animations, raster images and other multimedia elements, the sending and receipt of multimedia mail, and the easy creation of new Andrew packages, seamlessly in one user environment built under X Windows on UNIX. The Help System is designed to support the user more comprehensively than the basic man command. The system is set up to provide help on any of the programs that make up the Andrew Toolkit or the underlying UNIX system. To get help on any topic in the system the user first types the command "help which" displays a window (see Figure 7.8 Andrew Help Screen) listing the main programs on which help is available in the right side of the window. This list can be expanded to list all the programs for which help can be found by selecting an option from the menus.

Help can be found by using a specific word which describes something the user wants, such as 'Bitmap,' or a specific program, such as 'ez.' The system can also maintain a history of the help requests made by the user (see Figure 7.9 Andrew Help Screen 2). This allows the user to backtrack through the help screens they have accessed and thus follow-up keywords or return to previously viewed information.

This system better supports the user than the standard command, since the users are choosing a subject they require from a list of meaningful options rather trying to guess at what might be the correct term. There are *overview documents* that can give the user an overview of what each available topic is, rather than the user having to wade through a series of entries to find out whether it is like the one line description. The system also incorporates manual pages defined to a strict format which is designed to allow the user to find specific sections quickly without having to read the whole entry and contains a section on related topics in the system. To view any of these related topics, or if at any time a term in the text is not understood, it can be highlighted with the mouse and the system will attempt to find an entry explaining that term.

A similar program, called 'xman,' has been developed for the standard UNIX system. It too lists all the available commands, but this command is in addition to and optional to the standard 'man' system and not the de facto system as 'help' is for Andrew, as well as providing fewer features.

Figure 7.8–Andrew Help Screen: This screen shows the large left-hand window which displays the help page for the users chosen topic, here the start-up contents of 'help.' On the right are two smaller windows showing document titles on general aspects of the system in 'Overviews' and a list of the programs available under Andrew in 'Program.'

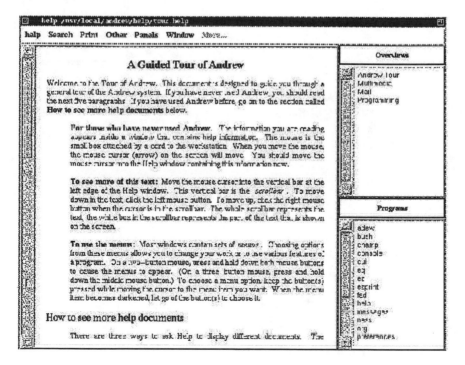

Figure 7.9–Andrew Help Screen 2: This shows the history window in the bottom right hand corner, showing the programs on which the user has sought help.

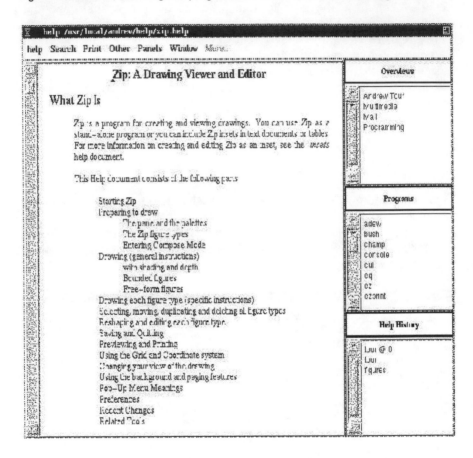

Web

The World Wide Web provides an interface to libraries like the world has never seen previously. The web provides a massive collection of retrieval tools that expedite finding information anywhere on the web. Features of tools that were originally developed independently of the web and operated independently of it have become incorporated rapidly into features of web systems. For instance, Gopher had much wider usage than the web for some years. That's no longer true and whatever can be done with Gopher is now done through a web interface and typically more easily.

The WAIS information servers at one point competed with the web for information access provision, but the word frequency tools used by WAIS are now part of web retrieval tools.

Aside from these generic interfaces to web information, one can go via the web to specific sites for retrieving software-related assets. For instance, the United States Army maintains an active web site for the "Army Reuse Center." There one can not only learn much about the Army's views on reuse, but can also gain access to depositories of software assets (see Figure 7.10 Army Center).

Figure 7.10–Army Center: This screen image shows the web-based tutorial to the Army Reuse Center reusable software library (Army, 1997).

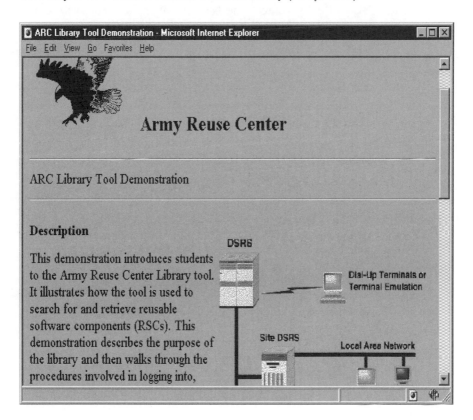

Asset Source for Software Engineering Technology (ASSET) was originally constituted by the Defense Advanced Research Projects Agency as a sub-task under the Software Technology for Adaptable Reliable Systems program to provide an on-line repository for reusable software. Its first four years were devoted to developing, operating, and maintaining the systems needed to operate the repository. In 1995, Science Applications International Corporation (SAIC) began transitioning ASSET to a commercial site on the World Wide Web. SAIC/ASSET's core capabilities and experience, therefore, are centered around software reuse and web technology: digital libraries, database management, object-oriented systems development, software configuration management, distributed information systems and Internet/Web-based telecommunications.

SAIC/ASSET offers products and services over the web on the topic of software reuse. One of its divisions is called Worldwide Software Resource Discovery. That division contains over 1,000 assets available to the public via the World Wide Web. From the web site users can search, browse and download assets cataloged in 38 domains. Another division of SAIC/ASSET is called Reusable Software Asset Brokerage Services. This service provides access to commercial high-technology software and tools via an electronic commerce service. Users may search, browse, and order directly from the Web site (see Figure 7.11 SAIS/ASSETS). Vendors with tools for sale can directly add their products to the SAIC/ASSET catalog.

Monitoring Retrieval

If items retrieved from the library are separated into 'relevant' and 'non-relevant' sets (see Figure 7.12 Retrieved Sets), then Recall and Precision may be defined:

- *Recall* measures the ability of a system to retrieve relevant documents,
- While conversely, *precision* measures the ability to reject non-relevant materials.

Alternatively, recall can be viewed as sensitivity and precision as accuracy.

Figure 7.11–SAIS/ASSET: This screen from the company SAIS/ASSET shows some assets retrievable through its web site. The library is organized in various ways. The path to this site went from domains to artificial intelligence.

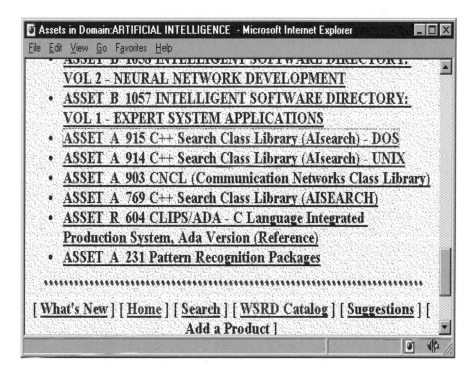

A good system is one which exhibits both high recall and high precision. A mathematical model of recall versus precision has been described and can be used to quantify the *trade-off* in recall and precision (Gordon and Kochen, 1989). In general most systems with high recall have low precision, and most high precision systems have relatively low recall.

The *size of a library* relates to its value. The larger the stock of a library the more likely the library is to contain the desired component. The retrieval effort pays off more often and thus is more likely to be used by developers to find components. The larger the library is the more it will cost to build, but use of the library will be more cost effective due to cost savings resulting from reusing components. There must be a trade-off between these requirements. Policies can be defined for adding components to the library. The library retrieval system could be set up to monitor requests for components and produce statistics for the rate of retrieval for each of the components in the library. This will show which types of components are the most useful in the library and thus should be updated or expanded. If the library system also produces statistics based on components that are requested but do not exist in the library, the library organizers could monitor which components should be added. If a well organized method is used to search the library, the failed searches could provide detailed specifications of needed components.

Figure 7.12–Retrieved Sets: Definitions of measures for retrieval performance.

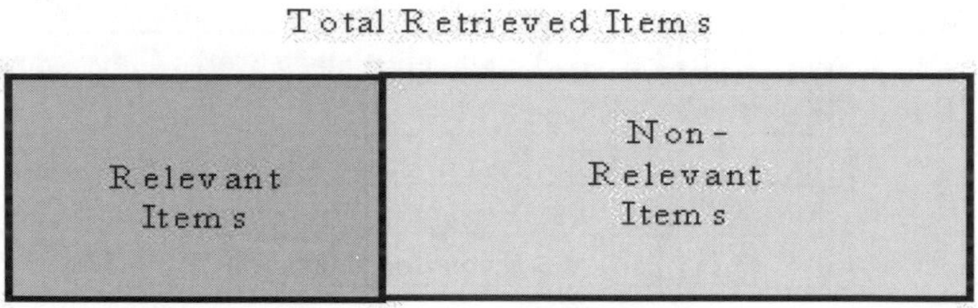

Total Retrieved Items

Relevant Items	Non- Relevant Items

$$Recall = \frac{Number\ of\ items\ retrieved\ and\ relevant}{Total\ relevant}$$

$$Precision = \frac{Number\ of\ items\ retrieved\ and\ relevant}{Total\ retrieved}$$

Epilogue

The concept of retrieving documents from a library is intrinsically linked with that of storing the data in the library. Software documents communicate some model of the world, and for reuse of these concepts a developer needs to be able to access this model.

The user of a software reuse library is assisted in searching for useful software components by an *information retrieval system* (see Figure 7.13 Principle of Information Retrieval from User Perspective). Using document-oriented techniques a searcher enters keywords to specify a software document. These retrieval methods, though simple, can work well. But semantically they are very weak, and there can be little structure implied in a search. In the object-oriented perspective, domain analysis is used and software components are seen as objects with attributes, including 'input,' 'output' and 'function.' The user then searches for useful components by specifying desirable attribute values. This method is more flexible for retrieval than document-oriented techniques, but results in the organization of the library being more difficult and time-consuming to set up and maintain. The user has a need for a component or components, this need is expressed by them to the Information Retrieval System, which can obtain the components.

Document-oriented retrieval requires that the user has a firm idea of both what his or her desired component looks like, and how it is likely to have been described or indexed at the organizational stage by either a human or automatic indexer. This contradicts one of the basic requirements of a software component system, that the user of the library must be able to retrieve a software component even when their ideas of how it might work precisely are not yet fully formed or defined. This makes retrieval particularly difficult for a developer in the early stages of the software development life-cycle, when he or she may most need to know which reusable components are available to fulfill his or her needs, and thus this is another factor discouraging to potential users. This method may also be a problem for the novice user, who may not easily be able to express his or her needs clearly due to inexperience of the domain or of the retrieval system.

The *object-oriented retrieval* methods are more formal and require more effort from the people building the library. Domain modeling must take place each time a component is to be added to the library, as the model must be carefully maintained to ensure its integrity. Thesauri are very useful tools to support retrieval but they too require much human effort to create and maintain.

Traditionally there is a *tension.* A system is either large, complex, and difficult to maintain but supports complex and powerful searching techniques for users, with facilities such as a thesaurus. However if the thesaurus is not well presented by the retrieval system, then this is an extra factor to bewilder and discourage novice users. Or a system is essentially very simple and it is up to the user to work out how to find the components they need. This tension has been a contributing factor to the lack of acceptance of software reuse as a standard practice in software development in the software industry.

The wide-spread use of the *World Wide Web* has changed many things. The web does not resolve the problem of building thesauri. If anything the plethora of information on the web makes the importance and challenge of good organization and thesauri all the more severe. However, the popularity of the web interface creates a certain uniformity of expectation and use that supports the use of web libraries. Even simple domain models and free text searching can be good enough when the assets are good and people are comfortable with the interface.

Figure 7.13–Principle of Information Retrieval from User Perspective: The user has a need for a components, this need is expressed to the information retrieval system which can obtain the components.

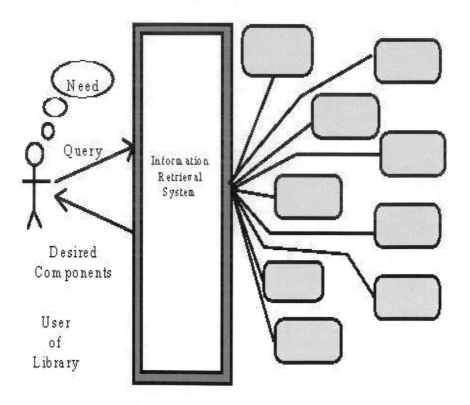

Chapter 8
Reorganizing

The goal of software reuse is not simply to find program and document components which might subsequently be reused, it is also to allow the developer to modify and combine components and concepts to create new software. In general, the components and concepts retrieved by the software developer from the library cannot be directly reused without being modified. They must be revised to fit with the target problem. This stage may be called *asset utilization* or *reorganization*. How much work is needed to reorganize an item depends upon many factors.

If the library contains program code for reuse, then unless the components were designed from the outset to be reused in other projects and in other domains, then reorganizing the component may not be a simple case of instantiating the existing general component for the current problem in hand. Fundamental changes to a component may be necessary. For example, to change the data-type or language, a redesign may be required. Alternatively, the library may contain the top-level design documents abstracted from the brief of the prior project. These are general documents and changing aspects of them is easier than with more specific documents, but the number of *abstractional stages* that are reused is reduced.

The application in which the component was originally developed will affect it in many ways, some perhaps extremely subtle. In a particular application it may be important for a component to be efficient in its memory allocation, or to be fast and efficient in execution. This is just one of many compromise decisions that may be encoded in a software document, be it a code segment or a design document. There may be many *compromises* made in the design of the software, dealing with every aspect of the described component: usability versus functionality, readability versus optimization, and so on. These must be transformed to match the developers current application. This can be extremely difficult to do, and is made more difficult by the fact that the original developers themselves may not have been aware of some decisions of this type.

Retrieved Component Suitability

Even if a search for an item does not simply fail, the retrieved item may not fit the *expectations* of the developer. To what this may be attributable will depend on the skills and methodologies of both the indexer and the developer. Systems for retrieval might allow searches to account for quality of desired components. Items may be inefficient or poorly tested.

A code segment or design, although well written may have requirements for control over data structures or system resources that are unreasonable in the context of the new target system. As a simplified example, a retrieved item may be a fast sorting algorithm. However to operate this algorithm requires two copies of the data. This may be undesirable, or infeasible given storage restrictions on the target machine.

The library may only store components expressed in one design methodology or programming language (or both). However if *mixed methodologies* are used, it might be the case that a retrieved component is expressed in a specification or programming language with which the developer is unfamiliar. If this is the case it may be that the developer cannot rely on understanding the component to the required degree. Only in extreme circumstances would it be considered worthwhile for the developer to learn a new software engineering technique, or programming language in order to comprehend the component. A similar problem would exist if the library contained specifications which were a mixture of dataflow oriented and control-flow oriented designs, as these are fundamental methodologies and cannot easily be reconciled together.

It may be very clear to a developer that a component exactly fits the specification, or is totally *unsuitable*. However in most cases the usefulness of the retrieved component or components is somewhere between these two extremes. It would be ideal if some automatic system could be designed to quantify how close a match exists between the retrieved component or components and the desired one. This is a non-trivial exercise and could only be achieved (if at all) by complex and formal specification of both the retrieved components and the target component, which would in many cases be undesirable.

The common method for modifying code is to thoroughly read the code and from that design and implement the modifications. Problems are found and usefulness assessed by the time-consuming process of modification itself. Also in many cases it will not be simply a case of closely examining a single component. If the library system is large and well stocked then it may return, superficially useful components. All or some of them may be suitable for the target component, some may even be optimal, but to analyze them to the level required to illicit this information is difficult and time-consuming.

It has been a common theme in this book that in the creation of any software component, design decisions have been made by the original designer that affect the component and it's reusability. These *design decisions* fall into roughly three categories :

1. Those that describe the problem domain and model the solution,
2. Constraints imposed by the solution space, such as power and type of target machine and programming language used, and
3. Stand alone decisions that have little or no effect on the rest of the program.

Decisions of Type 1 are the most important ones in the reuse process, these are affected by Type 2 decisions. Type 3 are in general irrelevant. Some design decisions are explicitly documented, though usually these will only be the fundamental decisions that affected large areas of the components structure. Most decisions made and in many cases, all decisions, go undocumented and thus the reason that the decision was made and to a large extent the specific result of that decision are lost. The only representation of the decisions is the parts of the program that were influenced by the decision made. These parts may be hidden in several parts of the program and influenced by other factors and decisions.

So it is important to be able to find these hidden global and local decisions. These are most detectable at different levels of abstraction. The major decisions are best viewed at a higher level of abstraction than a representation suitable for finding the localized decisions. *Reverse engineering* is helpful in this process, it is the process of extracting a higher level description of a component from a lower level one, such as pseudo-code from a C code program (Hausler *et al*, 1990). Performing this task reveals decisions that are obscured by the perhaps pages of code that is required to implement them (Ruigaber *et al*, 1990).

Document Reorganizing

Reorganization of *non-code documents* forms an important part of utilizing reusable components since much of the information generated by the software development cycle produces critical documents as well as the next abstraction of the algorithm. Some of this documentation will be created anew, but for the reused components attempts should be made to generate the new documents from their existing documentation (see Figure 8.1 Document Reorganization)

Figure 8.1–Document Reorganization: Original documents are processed using their outlines and thesauri to form new outlines and thus new documents.

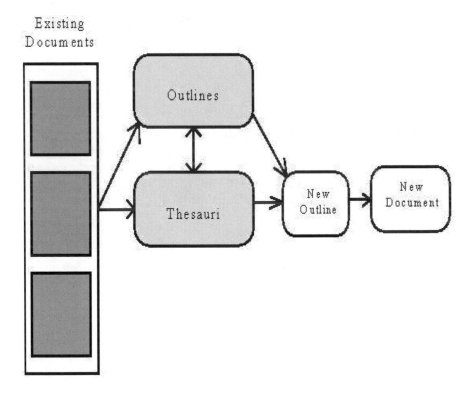

Figure 8.2–Document Reorganization Using a Thesaurus: The documents are indexed using common terms, shown in the large box above. Those documents that share indexing terms can be considered to cover some common ground and thus are candidates for integration.

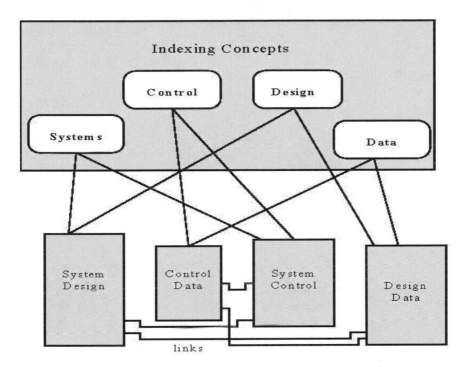

A single document can be reorganized by moving around its sections. To be able to do this in a meaningful and constructive way requires that the outline and document be designed in a carefully balanced and modular manner (Rada, 1990). There are problems however with simply changing the ordering of a document. Good documents present an argument and then gradually develop that argument as they progress. Simply re-sorting a group of paragraphs will destroy this *cohesiveness*.

Components from several documents can be reorganized together forming a new document. This can be performed by searching for blocks of text containing certain key words, whereupon the outlines they are part of are combined and reduced to allow the user to form a new document. *Thesauri* are useful in aiding the reorganization of documents. If two documents have been indexed using some or all of the same terms, then it is not unreasonable to assume that those two sections cover related topics and thus could be usefully compared or combined (see Figure 8.2 "Document Reorganization Using a Thesaurus"). If not enough links are generated by the raw indexing material, this method of concatenation can be extended by using a thesaurus to broaden the range of the linked terms.

Program Reorganizing

Retrieved software components may be modified in various ways (Mili *et al*, 1994):

- *specializing*: a generic component is in some way made specific to the current problem,

- *composing*: reusable components are reassembled to satisfy new requirements.

- *tailoring*: adaptation of software components for new requirements.

Tailoring is the rewriting of an existing component to meet a desired specification and was discussed earlier in this book under the heading of 'Asset Utilization.' Tailoring is labor intensive and discourages the reuser in that many of the required tasks, such as in-depth analysis of existing code, are unpleasant and tedious.

Specialization

Specialization is the act of binding generic components to the desired solution space. For this to be effective the programming language used for the components must support generalized constructs. Ada provides structured techniques for generic components, called *generic packages* (see Figure 8.3 Generic Variables). The package is instantiated in the main code segment of a program that uses this package. A package may even be instantiated for more than one data type within the same program. This is made possible by Ada's ability to handle overloaded operators. For example, there can be several versions of the function add_item, all called add_item. When a call to add_item is made the version of add_item instantiated to use the correct variable type for the calling parameters is automatically selected.

In other languages, depending upon the complexity of the data structure to be inserted or modified, search and replace techniques or conditional compilation methods support specialization. *Conditional compilation* is a method in which a makefile, a file that controls the compilation of perhaps several separate source files to produce an object program, contains conditional statements. By setting variables, the makefile will compile different versions of a program. For example, on some systems several separate code routines exist to drive different visual display units (different number of colors, size of screen, and such). Any program which is to drive the display on any specific machine will have a variable set to indicate which display it has and the makefile will detect this, based on environmental variables, and automatically compile the correct display device driver.

Another kind of generic instantiation is *template* based. Here a program code routine is written containing blank spaces, where for example the declarations should go. To instantiate the routine all the user needs to do is fill in the blanks (see Figure 8.4 Template). This offers advantages over simple code modification in that the area that needs to be modified is highlighted for the developers, and thus they do not have to spend a long time trying to analyze the function to find these areas themselves. The disadvantage of this method is that the templates must be specially created, either from scratch or derived from existing components.

Composition

Composition is the combination of separately designed and written components to create a cohesive whole, as in the UNIX pipe mechanism. When *composing components* it is important that they can be made to fit together correctly, i.e., that the parameters the first component passes to the second match the parameters that the second component expects from the first. In the UNIX pipe system, which is described in detail below, each program has just one input and one output; however, in most cases this is insufficiently powerful.

In the UNIX command line shell environment, standard system primitive commands are implemented as simple programs, such as 'lp' which prints a file, and 'cat' which opens a file and prints the contents to the screen. Each of these programs is small and provides only a limited functionality. However, when combined together using pipes, they can produce complex results.

Figure 8.3–Generic Variables: This code skeleton defines a package to implement an abstract data type for a queue. The items in the queue are defined as generic, and limited private (which is a code hiding technique to prevent users from attempting to 'hack' the internal structure of the package and misuse the provided functions). The queue itself is then defined to use those generic parameters. Nowhere in this code segment is a specific data type mentioned.

```
generic
    type item is private;
package queue_adt is
    type queue is limited private;

    -- Operators
    procedure add_item(to_queue:queue;new_item:item);

    -- Conditions
    function queue_empty(test_queue:queue)return boolean;

    private
    -- Code to implement the procedures and functions.

end queue_adt;
```

Every component has the same input and output mechanism, and the output of one can be joined to the input of another very simply using a simple command called a 'pipe.' To join two commands together is simply a case of placing the pipe command '|' between the two commands (see Figure 8.5 UNIX Pipe). This means that if a program is required to, for example, open a file, process it (for example to add certain components), and print the result, instead of a new program being written, or even a sequence of code modules being joined together and compiled, the three programs are simply linked together at the command line (see Figure 8.6 Inter-Program Communication Using Pipe). This forms what is called a 'pipeline.'

Figure 8.4–Template: An example of a code template, showing the parameters in bold that should or could be changed by the reusing developer.

```
Function BubbleSort (                          :arrays)
+ Template written by Andy Gray.

+ Declare Parameters :

+ Define first element of array
first_input :=

+ Define size of input array
length_input :=

Begin
      for counter_var = first_input  to  length_input-1
      + Check for counter_var element greater than next
      if
      then
            + Swap the items
      endif
end
```

Figure 8.5–UNIX Pipe: The process on the left takes its input, from Std-In and produces its output on Std-Out. The 'pipe' connects the Std-Out from Process One and the Std-In from Process Two. Thus the output from Process One becomes the input to Process Two.

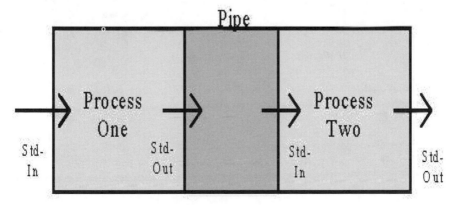

The developer is only required to write the 'new_process' part, the printer routine and file opening are supplied as part of the operating system. This means that the developer need only concern himself or herself with the new code, to actually calculate the totals. Input and output to the new routine are dealt with using simple input and output code, which is similar to the code that would be used outside the pipe environment. This allows for massive increases in reliability, since 'cat' and 'lp' will already have been in use with many other programs and have therefore already have been implemented for the current system and exhaustively tested.

Figure 8.6–Inter-Program Communication Using Pipe: 'cat' opens the file and its output is fed (via a pipe) into 'new_process' input and then 'new process' output is fed (again via a pipe) into 'lp's input.

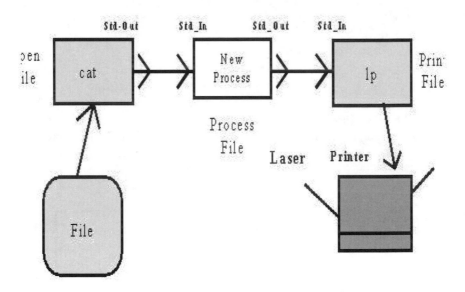

There is no problem with version numbers since the programs are not actually compiled together and all *versions* used will automatically be the latest one. UNIX provides several of these basic programs for opening files, printing them, sorting them, searching them, word counting, and so forth. Since the code used to implement these routines is very basic C code, and all UNIX systems use C, they should be very portable from system to system.

A very useful application of this pipe technique is to use programs as what are called *filters*. These are extensively used in many systems. For example, say that the totals program 'new_process' above, will only work with floating point numbers, due to the way in which it was written. It would be possible to modify the source code to create another program to add up integers, but this may be bad practice. For example, if the way in which the totals are calculated is changed, then the two programs, floats and integers, must be modified, not one. In UNIX one solution is to write a filter, another program which goes into the pipeline, that takes integers and converts them to floats. Thus only the pipeline is changed and 'new_process' is unmodified.

This filter technique can be and is used to solve common problems, such as that of picture display and conversion. Many different file formats exist for storing raster picture information. Many micro-computer platforms have their own most prevalent image formats, such as TIFF and PCX. Other formats are more common on workstations, such as Postscript encapsulated rasters and X Bitmaps. More recently standard cross-platform formats like GIF and JPEG have become widely used. These formats are all incompatible with one another. A program for displaying GIFs cannot display a PCX file and a X Bitmap viewer cannot display a GIF.

A user may have a display program for every format he or she uses, for example a X Bitmap display program, a TIFF display program and so forth. Each program must handle different screen displays and is usually quite complex. An alternative approach is to have a set of conversion programs. But converting files one at a time is tedious. It would be better to have a single display program that could handle all formats. However building such a large system is a huge task. With the UNIX pipe another alternative is available. The user has one complex display program, that can display for example Portable PixMap (PPM) files, and has a *conversion program* to convert JPEG to PPM, X bitmap to PPM, and so forth. Pipes filter the input file to create a generic image format and send that to the display program (see Figure 8.7 Image Conversion).

The UNIX pipe mechanism is easy to use due to it's simplicity, but this is also a problem. It is often important to pass many different *parameters* in different forms, such as complex, abstract data structures, like arrays, stacks or queues, for which the above is not an appropriate model. It is only suited to simple flows of information. The handling of complex parameters is greatly simplified in object-oriented languages, such as C++. Here the objects to be composed are distinct and communication between components is minimized to those values that make sense for a particular object.

Figure 8.7–Image Conversion: The original image format is filtered by a relevant program to produce a PPM or Portable PixMap. This is a very simple 'lowest common denominator' file format, which is easy to handle. Then this file is displayed via a pipe by another program which can only display PPM's, which performs all the complex display handling. A large number of programs are available to perform functions on PPMs, such as to double the size.

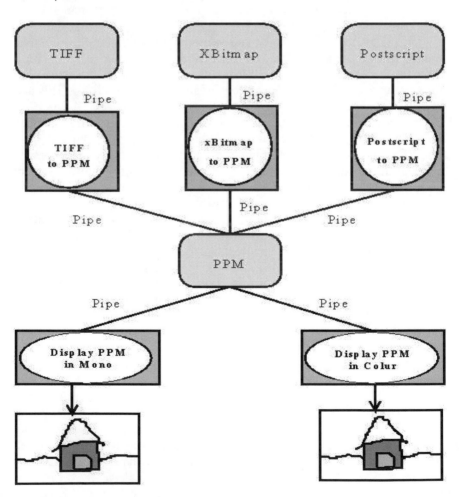

Work has been done on *Module Interconnection Languages* (DeRemer and Kron, 1976; Kaiser and Garlan, 1987) in which rules automate code level integration. Developers describe their software as a set of modules and a specification of each of their input and output characteristics. The system then tests the connections to see whether they are compatible. This approach to building reusable components makes relevant compromises between the granularity of the components and specificity of their function.

Code Generators

An alternative method of creating code efficiently is to generate it automatically from formal requirements or design. This code generation technique is not strictly speaking software reuse. On the other hand, it is another use of the specification and bypasses the organization and retrieval stages of the reuse cycle. The code generation approach may shorten the waterfall life-cycle by removing design, implementation, and testing from the software production process. Developers specify the desired program in some high-level language, with a possible mix of declarative and procedural constructs. The *generated programs* are usually correct in construction, thus alleviating the need for testing.

In some views of software engineering, software development is seen as simply a series of *transformations* (Balzer, 1981; Rich and Waters, 1988; Green and Westfold, 1982; Smith *et al*, 1985) from formal specifications to the finished program (see Figure 8.8 Program Transformation). Code generating systems are designed such that given a program specification written using some formal method, like Z-Schema or VDM, that specification is transformed, via a series of intermediate representations, to either an executable form or a form that can be readily made executable. Code generation systems have four main advantages:

1. They relieve developers from labor-intensive, routine derivation of the lower level abstractions of code.

2. Since the lower abstractions are machine generated, transcription mistakes are impossible,

3. The system automatically maintains a record of development choices, their rationale, or both, for maintenance purposes. Since this too is automatically generated it too is error free, and

4. Ensures the 'correctness' of the resulting programs by construction.

The transformation is performed by *syntactic rules* which work upon the original definition and replace it with lower-level abstractions, until the executable stage is reached (see Figure 8.9 Program Transformation). In a reuse scenario a transformation may also be required to modify an existing retrieved component specification that does not quite match the developer's specification into a specification to fulfill those requirements (Boyle *et al*, 1984).

Figure 8.8–Program Transformation: The formal specification is transformed via several intermediate representations to produce a target program, and a log of the changes made by each transformation is maintained.

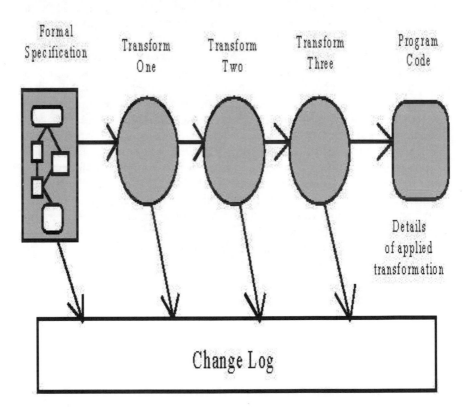

Figure 8.9–Program Transformation Example: Here can be seen part of a formal specification (in a textual form, for simplicity). This specifies that at that particular point the user may wish to load an example file. This can be transformed or expanded to show the tasks involved in the two intermediate representations (I.R. 1 and I.R. 2) choosing a file and opening the file. This in turn can be expanded to list the steps involved in each of these stages. This produces an executable specification, which could be compiled or perhaps transformed (via T'form 1 and T'form 2) into an executable language like C or Pascal.

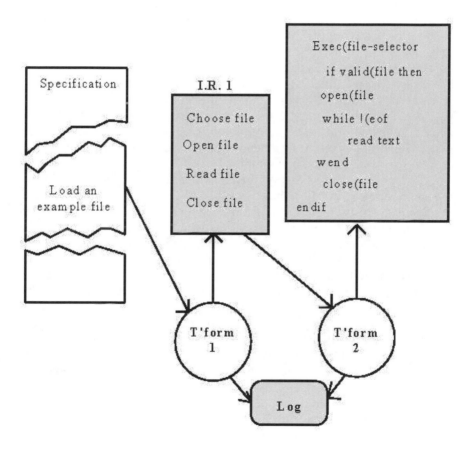

The difficulty in creating software using the transformation method is that the developer must specify exactly and with total accuracy his or her desired component using a complex, formal method. Furthermore, this method has not been successfully implemented on other than *toy*

examples and the amount of knowledge necessary to implement a system for anything larger could be prohibitive (Partsch and Steinbruggen, 1983).

Testing after Reuse

In the vast majority of cases software will not be reused in the same state in which it was retrieved from the library, instead it will be modified or re-written. These changes mean that any validation or testing techniques used to check the original program are no longer guaranteed to be applicable. This case is also true of programs that are modified as part of the normal software maintenance process, and it has been because of this that the selective revalidation of software has been most extensively researched in the past. This technique involves designing *testing strategies* that instead of testing a program exhaustively, which has already been fully tested prior to being modified, simply tests the modified sections. This is quite complex as the interactions between perhaps hundreds of components are extremely complex.

However in a reuse situation this revalidation is more complex due to the more subtle ways in which the original testing procedures can be *invalidated*. For example the original testing can be made invalid by the component being reused in a situation where the data the routine is required to act upon is different in emphasis and range of values.

Reuse provides special challenges to a developer who reaches the testing stage. Testing is easier to do if the developer of a piece of software is at hand, since that individual will know that piece of software intimately and will have a good idea of what they think are difficult parts of the solution that the program provides. In many ways of course it could be argued that equally important is to use an impartial tester who does not have a large set of preconceived ideas about how the routine is written and what special cases and so forth are handled in the code. However, in a reuse scenario the choice of using either or both will not exist in many cases, since the original developer of a reused component might have no connection at all with the current team. The program may come with test data, but if the program has been changed, then this test data may be inappropriate. The programmer or analyst who has modified the component will obviously have gained an understanding of the component, but this will not usually be as in depth as that held by its *original author*.

Whilst talking about software testing it is appropriate to talk about the quality of software. All through this book it has been put forward that the quality of a component is extremely important for the reusability of that component. But what is quality? Due to its subjective nature, quality is best enforced using guidelines for developers so that when a component is written it can be expected to have certain features that are considered to give *quality* to a component, such as all modules having approximately a standardized size and all having been tested using specific techniques and documented to a specified quality level (Halstead, 1977). This created software is then reviewed by someone other than the author to ensure that the standards have been followed (see Figure 8.10 Quality Review). This task is also performed when the software is modified in some way. Determining quality is a challenging and continuous task, as was also indicated in the 'Reuse Framework' Chapter.

Figure 8.10–Quality Review: From the original specification the developer creates a software package following the guidelines. The component is checked for quality by the reviewer comparing it with the guidelines and a review of how well it meets the criterion is written.

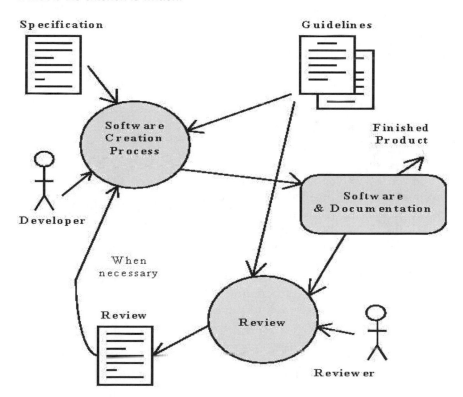

Epilogue

Precise methods for tailoring or adapting software or other assets are not generally useful. Instead the reorganization of assets remains largely an art. The analogy to reproduction with change in biology is partially valid. The *organisms* do not know exactly how to modify their genes, but use some broad heuristics like the cross-over operator and hope for the best. Software reuse is a little like this. The problems relate to the complexity of the assets to be reused and the complexity of the target, new products.

One recent experience highlights these difficulties. A team attempted to reuse three standard pieces (Garlan *et al*, 1995):

- an object-oriented database,
- a toolkit for constructing graphical user interfaces, and
- an event-based tool-integration mechanism.

Selection of assets to reuse was made on the basis of promise for working together and requiring the same compiler that the team used on its other major project. After five person years a prototype was developed, but the system was huge, sluggish, and difficult to maintain. The main difficulties resulting from the integration included:

- excessive code,
- poor performance,
- the need to modify external packages, and
- the need to reinvent existing functions.

In retrospect, the problems were largely associated with conflicting assumptions among the parts that were being reused. Each asset is based on certain assumptions, pre-eminently about the data model, the control model, the protocols, the topology of system communication, the presence of other components, and an order of operation. These assumptions are not typically made clear enough in an asset description. The reuse team discovers these assumptions the hard way as it tailors the assets to the new situation. Thus, successful tailoring must begin with careful selection of assets from a well-understood library of components that is harmonious in many ways with the environment of the new development team.

It is something of a *paradox* that the Reorganizing Stage is the most important of the entire reuse cycle, but is the least well covered in research and tools. There are several reasons for this. The first and foremost reason is that reorganization can not occur until there has been organization and retrieval and those two steps remain themselves the subject of much debate and research.

The organization and retrieval stages are based on much long term work in the field of library science. The reorganization stage enjoys no such parallel field. Reorganization is the most complex and difficult to perform. It will be no easier to automate this stage of the reuse process than to write programs which can themselves write programs, adapting to problems along the way.

The reorganizing stage raises many questions:

- If code is retrieved, is it in the right language? How well has this code been tested? Is the test data available?

- If design documents are retrieved, are they in the appropriate design language?

- If two components are retrieved that do the same job using different algorithms (for example merge and shell sorts), which is the most applicable here?

- Can documentation be reused too?

Many of these questions have no simple answer but the reorganization phase depends on answers to these questions.

Once reorganization is completed, it is then and only then that it is first possible for the development team to look back over the project and attempt to assess if reuse techniques have paid off in this project. There are many possible pay-offs that reuse may have, including shorter development time, less expertise demanded of team members, and greater reliability and number of components created for future reuse. Successful reorganization depends on good organization and retrieval. Additionally, no organization or retrieval can be good unless the ultimate reorganization is successful.

Section 4
Practical Examples

This section contains three chapters. The first describes reuse tools, while the second presents case studies in the management of reuse at companies. The third chapter is about systems for multimedia courseware reuse.

Chapter 9
Software Reuse Tools

Within this Chapter several prototype systems are examined which support document and object-oriented software reuse. First software engineering tools are reviewed and then two prototype reuse systems, called Practitioner and SoftClass. Finally a user interface generator is described.

CASE

Computer Aided Software Engineering (CASE) may increase productivity in software development. The productivity gained by using CASE comes from the following areas:

1. CASE tools help enforce consistent technique usage throughout an organization.
2. Interactive graphics support allows software engineers to develop and manage diagrams that help communicate design concepts.
3. CASE tools ease the complex book-keeping chores associated with software implementation through a system of reminders.

In order to maintain consistency throughout the software development cycle, many CASE tools have centrally a database that stores all the components of a project. This *database* must at the very least allow engineers to logically associate documentation and source code, annotate freely any part of the design, and manage different versions of the software in production. But, by it's very nature, a CASE environment will make further demands on a database. For example, it must allow simultaneous access by team members, allowing them to work independently and then merge their work back into the main project. Hypertext, with it's arbitrary information structuring and entity relationships, provides an appropriate model on which such a system may be built.

CASE Architectures

There are a great many CASE tools available which aid the software development process in a variety of ways. An *Integrated Project Support Environment* (IPSE) is intended to support all of the activities in the software process from initial feasibility studies to software maintenance and evolution. At present there are few IPSEs in use, but there are many under construction in North America, Europe and Japan. Several available software tools are interfaced to a database management system so that output of any one tool could potentially be an input into any other tool. It is normally the case that tool interaction is predictable, but there are many cases of serendipitous tool combinations and the IPSE database allows these combinations to occur when required. Another advantage is that the project management have direct access to project information and management tools and are able to use actual data collected during the course of the project (see Figure 9.1 Case Tools).

All of the documents produced in the course of a project from feasibility studies to fault reports can, if necessary, be put under configuration control and managed by the configuration management tools which are an integral part of the environment. Furthermore the database facilities are rich enough to allow relationships between documents to be recorded so that designs, for example, could be linked to their associated code, and changes to each automatically tracked. If an environment is properly *integrated*, all support tools will present the user with a consistent interface, so that the task of learning new tools would be made significantly easier.

A typical structure for IPSEs is to be built around a layered system, analogous to an onion, where there are a number of layers of functionality provided by the different levels in the system. The model includes the following layers.

1. Operating System,

2. Database System,

3. Object Management,

4. Public Tools Interface, and

5. User Interface.

Figure 9.1–Case Tools: The database supports the wider functions taking place in the development of software.

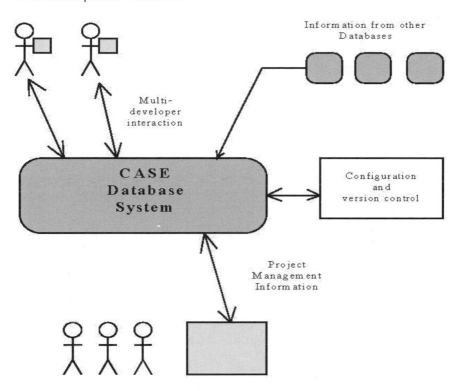

It can be argued that IPSEs should be built in conjunction with a special purpose *operating system* tailored to support the environment, but the need for portability has meant that the innermost kernel (layer 1) in the IPSE is a standard operating system. The majority of IPSEs have been chosen to be built on top of the UNIX operating system. The reasons for this are partly to make use of the software tools supported by UNIX.

The third layer in the IPSE is the layer which distinguishes an IPSE from a software toolkit or CASE workbench. This is the *object management* layer which is responsible for controlling and managing all of the entities produced during software development. Broadly, the object management layer allows objects to be named, to exist in a number of different versions, and it provides facilities for relationships to be recorded between objects.

Hypertext CASE

Many *interconnections* exist among the components of the software life-cycle but these interconnections are difficult and time-consuming to maintain in paper forms. Hypertext makes it practical to connect all these pieces together automatically and dynamically (Biggerstaff, 1989). Furthermore, hypertext supports information reuse. For example, when a paragraph about a component's design is used as a comment in the program documentation and as a paragraph in both the user and design documentation, in a conventional system this means creating and maintaining multiple copies of the same information. In hypertext, this configuration can be implemented with appropriate links from all the occurrences to a master copy of the information node. This gives many advantages, not the least being that any modifications made to the section are automatically reflected in all its occurrences. Also the relationship between such documents as requirements and code can be traced.

The *Hypertext Abstract Machine* (HAM) from Tektronix is a general-purpose hypertext storage system which can be used as a base engine for other hypertext systems and in CASE systems (Campbell and Goodman, 1988). HAM stores its database in a centralized file server. The storage model is based on five objects: graphs, contexts, nodes, links, and attributes. A graph is the highest-level object which, in turn, contains contexts. Each context has one parent context and zero or more child contexts. Contexts contain nodes and links, while attributes can be attached to contexts, nodes, or links. HAM is designed to work in a networked environment.

Tektronix has developed a CASE system called Neptune which uses HAM and is extensible (Delisle and Schwartz, 1986). Neptune holds all the project components : requirements, design, source code, test data and results, and documentation. In Neptune a link or node can have any number of *attribute/value pairs*. The attribute 'projectComponent' can have any value from the set of project components: requirements, design, source code, tests or documentation. The attribute 'relatesTo' is applied to links and can have any value from the set 'leadsTo,' 'comments,' 'refersTo,' 'callsProcedure,' 'followsFrom,' 'implements,' or 'isDefinedBy.' By example, a node with 'projectComponent' value of 'requirements' would have a 'relatesTo' value of 'leadsTo' with the node whose 'projectComponent' was 'design' (see Figure 9.2 Neptune).

A node may contain any amount or type of information. A link is not restricted to pointing to an entire node but can point to any point within a node. Contexts are defined by grouping nodes and links with certain values. For instance, nodes with the 'projectComponent' value of 'code' are implicitly grouped into a context and each node gets an attribute called 'System.' The values of 'System' can be UNIX or VMS a query is made for the node predicate of 'System=VMS,' then only those nodes whose source code is applicable to Digital Equipment Corporations VAX/VMS operating system are returned.

Figure 9.2–Neptune: Showing two nodes related by one attribute, as described in the text.

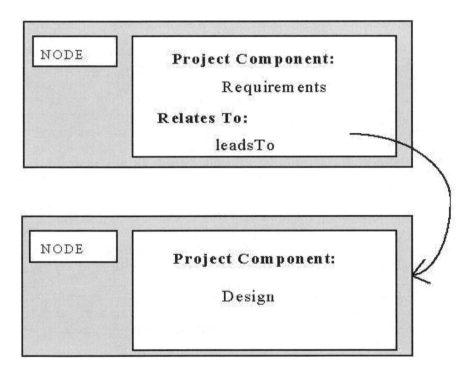

With Neptune one can copy a subset of nodes and links from one context into another context. Contexts can be used to define a workspace and partition a project into local and global *workspaces*. A local workspace lets a developer abstract a subset of nodes and links from the global workspace and place them in a workspace where he or she can make local modifications, test these modifications against the rest of the project, and when satisfied merge the changes back into the global workspace.

Ideally, the partitioning of workspaces between engineers should be disjoint, but in practice it may transpire that two or more are working on the same nodes concurrently. In order to allow this, Neptune must resolve concurrent update conflicts and not allow the work of one engineer to be overwritten by that of another when local workspaces are merged into the project workspace. To aid the developer in accessing all the information stored many browsers are available, these include a node browser, an attribute browser, a version browser and a node differences browser.

Practitioner

Practitioner was a five year project funded by the European Commission and comprising teams in Germany, the United Kingdom and Denmark. The ultimate goal was the development of a support system for developers involved in the pragmatic reuse of software concepts. This system was realized as a set of prototypes, called PRESS (*Practitioner Reuse Support System*). Practitioner was concerned with the reuse of software concepts from the 'ideas' embodied in requirements documents through to code.

PRESS was designed not to be bound to a specific programming language but to emphasize the description of software concepts. Thus it tried to bridge the gap between:

- knowledge representation techniques; and
- the more general, information storage and retrieval techniques, which are usually based around component retrieval from a library.

The PRESS system was designed with a 'domain specific application area' in mind, that of a Steel Mill, which the project used as its example, but embodied techniques that would be relevant in any area. To quote the project documentation:

'In a sense, the PRESS prototypes can be seen as an information platform for the trained professional in the technical world. They may be used not only to store and administrate information related to software concepts, but also more general domain-related information, about the application area the software was written for, in a structured form, which may be more or less rigorously formalized.'

Figure 9.3–Level One Press: Here the three main components of the system can be seen, in conjunction with their interactions with the user-interface.

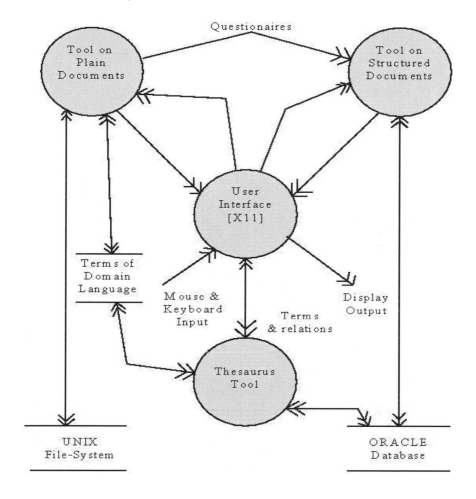

PRESS included three partially complementary prototypes: a small, low overhead variant called *PRESSTO*, a bigger and more powerful version called PRESSTIGE, and a collaborative hypertext system called MUCH. PRESSTO ran without any form of database system, being solely supported by the UNIX file system, whereas PRESSTIGE made substantial use of an SQL relational database management system.

Figure 9.4–ToPD Bubble: Tool on Plain Documents (ToPD) functionality.

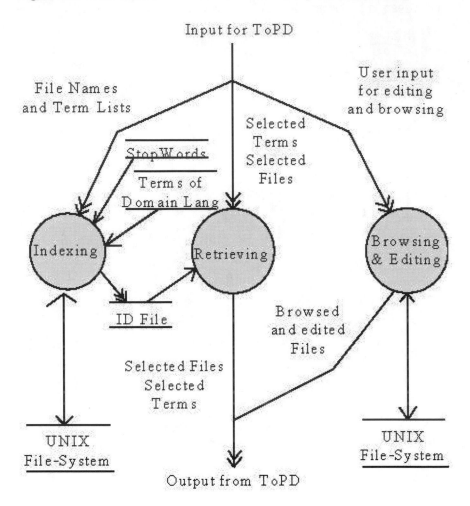

The *PRESS toolkit* included three processes exchanging information (see Figure 9.3 Level One Press). The `Tool on Plain Documents' was for retrieving plain text files based on words in them. The `Thesaurus Tool' and `Tool on Structured Documents' were for the manipulation of more structured information.

PRESSTO

PRESSTO is the simplest of the Practitioner tools, it is designed to specifically deal with plain text, with some thesaurus support. PRESSTO supports searching across document collections using words taken from a word index by the user. PRESSTO is very much based on features in the UNIX operating system and does not use a database system. PRESSTO instead simply accesses files containing reusable components or concepts as they are stored in directories on the host computer (see Figure 9.4 ToPD Bubble).

Figure 9.5–PRESSTO Indexer: Showing a document that has been loaded to be indexed and the functions that are available to act on it.

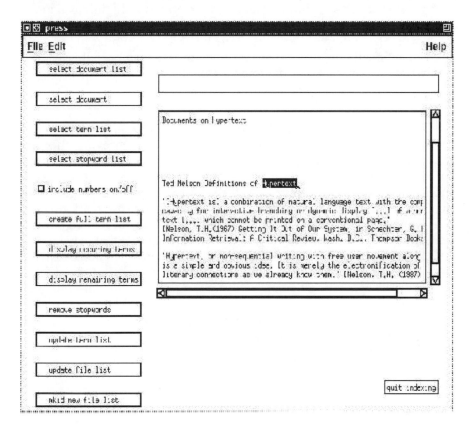

The key concept around which PRESSTO is built is the notion of the occurrence of a token (a term important to the developer) in a file. The main question that is being asked by a developer of the software is '*Which files contain which tokens?*.' To set up PRESSTO a file has to be created, called a 'ls-file' which lists all the relevant files containing reusable information and a 'talc-file' that lists all the relevant indexing words in a natural language (such as English or German). PRESSTO can then be used to extract all user defined symbols from programs written in a programming language such as C or to extract only those terms that appear in the talc and a document. The activation of the indexing function is controlled from a menu-based interface (see Figure 9.5 PRESSTO Indexer).

The *retrieval function* of the PRESSTO tool involves (see Figure 9.6 PRESSTO Retrieval) two modes, `File Mode' and `Index Term Mode.' In Index Term Mode clicking on an index term, for example `Giraffe,' causes all files that contain giraffe as an indexing term to be highlighted in the file list. Clicking on the file name then causes it to be displayed in the text window at the bottom of the screen. The File Mode is similar in principle but is functionally opposite. Hence clicking on a filename would cause all keywords contained in that file to be highlighted in the terms list.

PRESSTIGE

PRESSTIGE provides methods and tools for building a concept model called a 'questionnaire,' and provided techniques for retrieving information relating to software concepts. One method used to provide a structured form for entering information about software is to create a concept model. One of the main purposes of the concept model is to guide the analysis of documents being added and the extraction of the information that will be needed to reuse the component later in a structured way. A *concept model* should ideally contain all the information that may be useful to a potential reuser (Albrechtsen, 1990). It may be possible to derive some aspects of the concept model automatically using facilities offered by software engineering tools. The concept model should store information about itself in addition to the information it stores about the component it describes. It should say who created the concept model, if it is tied to a specific project, and so on. PRESSTIGE offered a set of supporting functions for three tasks :

Figure 9.6–PRESSTO Retrieval: The PRESSTO search tool interface. More power can be given by using the buttons in the middle of the screen. If two terms are selected, then clicking on 'OR' will list all files that contain either keyword, clicking on 'AND' would display all files that contain both. The 'NOT' button is designed to allow the developer to search for files that do not contain a particular term/set of terms.

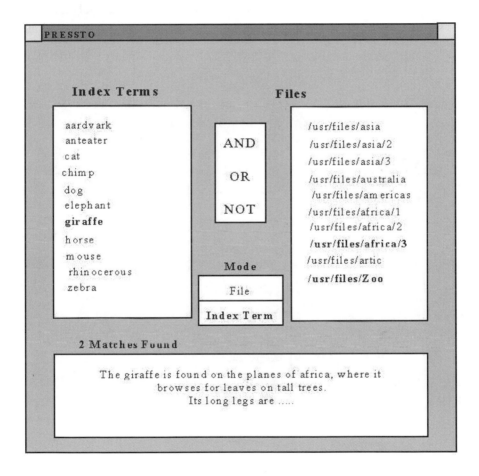

Figure 9.7–Hierarchical Concept Model: The answers to the questions on the 'Top Level' questionnaire are in turn 'Component 6,' 'String Lib,' 'Math Lib' and for 'Component 6,' 'A.D.T. 6.' This provides a hierarchically structured semantic net-like structure of descriptions of a software item.

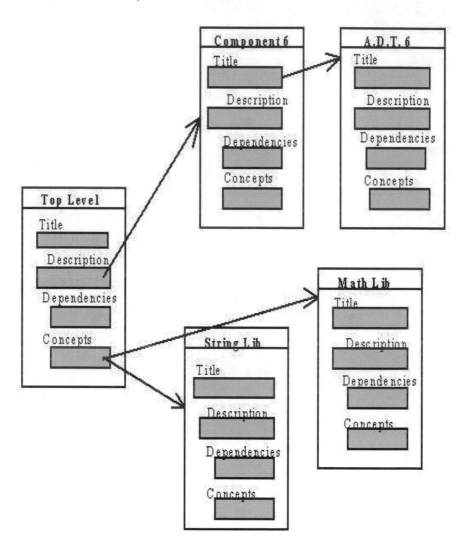

Figure 9.8–HLQS DFD: Data-Flow diagram of the software module. HLQS has
the three components Translate, Query, and Report.

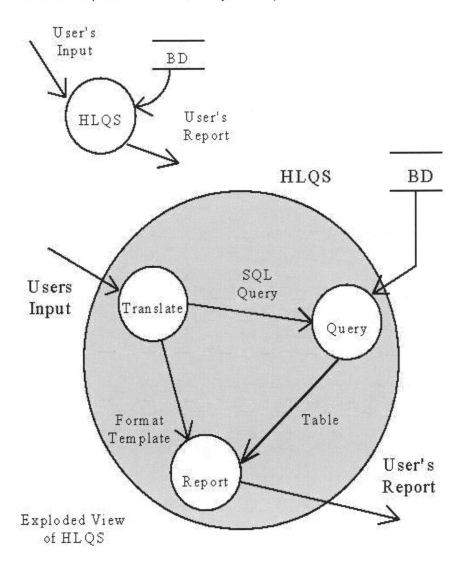

Figure 9.9–HLQS Concept Model: Excerpts from questionnaire describing HLQS.

```
High Level Interface to a Relation DBMS (HLQS)
Authorising Person: Joe Blow
Created by Person: John Smith
...
Definition:
Function: HLQS provides a high level interface...
Interfaces
Interfaces Provided
      User's report
Interfaces Required
      User's Input
      Relational DB
Concept Decomposition
Subconcept being Instantiated
      Translate
      Interface Bindings
      External concept interface bindings
                IN: User's Input
            Internal subconcept interface bindings
                OUT: SQL query
                OUT: Format template
Subconcept being Instantiated
      Query
      Interface Bindings
            External concept interface bindings
                IN: Relational DB
            Internal subconcept interface bindings
                IN: SQL Query
                OUT: Table
Subconcept being Instantiated
      Report
      Interface Bindings
            External concept interface bindings
                OUT: User's Report
            Internal subconcept interface bindings
                IN: Table
                IN: Format template
```

- Construction and maintenance of a thesaurus and its related indexing terms,

- Description and indexing of software concepts (using questionnaires), and

- Browsing and retrieval of software concepts.

These tasks constitute a reuse scenario, where the domain model provides a standard vocabulary that can be applied for subject representation (indexing) as well as for subject retrieval of software concepts. The *thesaurus links* together questionnaires and aids the developer in browsing groups of related documents by creating networks of documents based on linking terms in separate texts via the thesaurus.

The key components in the PRESSTIGE *questionnaire* are derived by the developer answering various questions about the component to be stored. What these questions are in a particular company would depend on the domain in which the PRESSTIGE system was to be used. Typical ones include :

- administrative to the questionnaire itself; such as 'authorizing person,' 'created by person' and 'date of creation,' or

- interfaces that the concept makes with other concepts, such as 'interfaces provided (output),' 'interfaces required (input),' and 'interface bindings.'

One of the main purposes of the questionnaire is to guide the analysis of the source material and the knowledge analysis process that finally leads to the formulation of reusable concepts. Questionnaires include Application-Oriented Descriptions, Implementation-Oriented Descriptions, and Historic Development (for version control) information. A questionnaire may reference another questionnaire. Allowing hierarchies of questionnaires allows a top-down decomposition of software concepts of any size, anything up to entire software systems (see Figure 9.7 Hierarchical Concept Model).

Questionnaires may be formed from scratch based on information in the software engineer's mind, or may be derived from existing software documents, such as programs or design documents. Filling in a questionnaire requires comprehension of the domain framework, especially when dealing with high-level conceptual designs. In many cases the questionnaire *attribute values* are uncontrolled, free text, but they can be the names of other questionnaires, providing a structured document tree. This is a mixed approach to library organization, i.e., a combination of both object (the questionnaires) and document (the answers on the questionnaires) methods.

Figure 9.10–The Base Window of the Search Tool: This window shows the Press search tool. An example of the result of a search for all the concept models indexed on `heating' is shown. The names in the window are the titles of concept models found using that term.

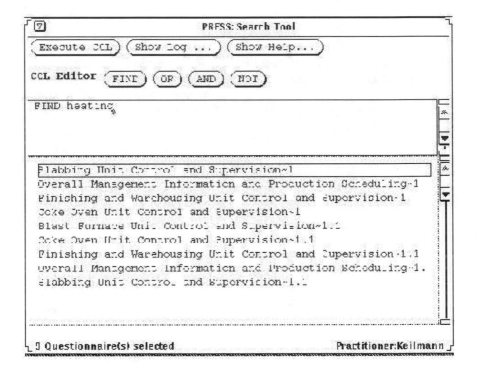

An example questionnaire will be provided for a software module that provides a high-level interface called HLQS to a relational database management system. HLQS takes as input a high-level query in some format, and accesses a database of records (see Figure 9.8 HLQS DFD). In the corresponding questionnaire (see Figure 9.9 HLQS Concept Model) the subcomponents are referred to only by name because it is expected that they be described in separate questionnaires. Interface

Bindings describe both the interface of the subcomponents to outside components (through the interface of the component itself) and the bindings to data flows that are internal to HLQS.

The PRESSTIGE search tool makes use of the Common Command Language (CCL) search language. The user is allowed the use of AND, OR, NOT and wild cards except that under PRESSTIGE they are used for the retrieval of questionnaires, not files (see Figure 9.10 The Base Window of the Search Tool). The form of a CCL statement is:

find [<property>=] <search term [+<thes. relations>]
[AND | OR | NOT [<property>=] <search term> [+<thes.
relations>]] [AND | OR | NOT ...

Where entries between brackets are optional search terms may contain wild cards. For example, the search term

ind?

will find questionnaires that have been indexed with a term starting with 'ind' such as indexing, indexed, or indices. The qualifier can constrain the matches found by a search by specifying a questionnaire property (for example the `Function' of component) for which the match must occur. The qualifier <thes. relations> is used to extend search terms. For example, the query:

find 'Function' = 'open-loop control' +BT

returns questionnaires whose Function have been indexed by `open-loop control' or any of its broader terms (BT).

The browse tool enables the user to see all the keywords from all the questionnaires, all authors of the concept models, all dates of creation of concept models, and so on. It allows the user to see the terminology used in all the questionnaires and thus get a flavor for the whole system. The form of a questionnaire for a domain can be described in any way the user chooses. Once a questionnaire has been set up, the questionnaires to be entered into the same system must be consistent with it. Once the Questionnaire Tool has retrieved a questionnaire the developer may edit it, copy it, delete it, or move it. The thesaurus tool is used for general management of the thesaurus (see Figure 9.11 PRESSTIGE Thesaurus Tool). A term, for example `open loop control,' can be entered and the thesaurus item for this term is retrieved and displayed in the ten windows that form the thesaurus tool display. The user can then see the BT (broader term), the date of creation, and so forth. Any of the terms generated by the search, for example the Narrower Term, can now be used as a search term to retrieve further related items. Usually only the domain analyst has control over adding and deleting terms to or from the thesaurus. Control over terms is important, if consistency is to be maintained throughout the thesaurus.

Figure 9.11–PRESSTIGE Thesaurus Tool: This is a tool to show a thesaurus term, in this case 'open-loop control,' and its associated terms.

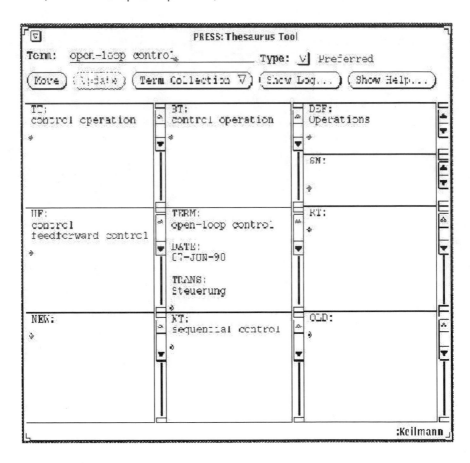

Figure 9.12–Practitioner Reuse Mill: This diagram shows how the different programs that were developed for the Practitioner project fit together and exchange information.

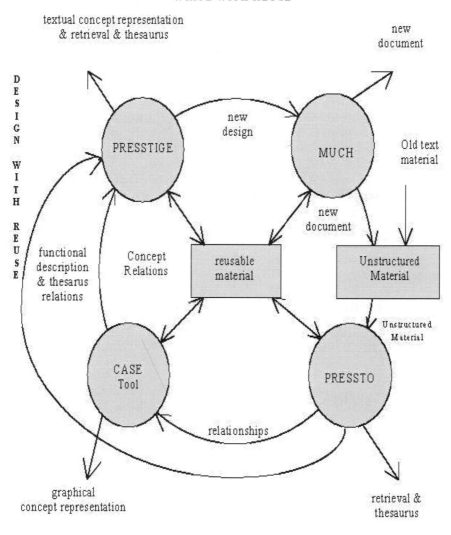

MUCH

The *MUCH* (Many Using and Creating Hypermedia) system supports collaborative hypertext authoring (Rada *et al*, 1989). MUCH enhances a number of functionalities of PRESS and helps integrate PRESSTO and PRESSTIGE into a single multi-faceted system (see Figure 9.12 Practitioner Reuse Mill). PRESSTO testing demonstrated that `understanding' tasks were not well-supported when searching separate, but inter-connected documents, the user having to go to the next one via word search. The MUCH system can alleviate the problems in this situation. The MUCH system is programmed in C running on networked UNIX workstations, having its own database system, and X-Windows interface.

MUCH puts stress on the *outline* in a document, since it forms the existing structure in documents and is possible to extract automatically. Outlines can provide an overview of a domain and can aid a user in domain exploration. In MUCH, a fisheye view of a document is implemented, by the user `folding/unfolding' the outline. Different links can be distinguished by labels. Annotation and discussion are also supported by a 'typed link,' called 'Comment' as a communication mechanism among co-authors. Users can add links between hypertext nodes at will (see Figure 9.13 Create Link). The MUCH system is particularly useful for *writing with reuse*. To this end two particularly strong features have been incorporated into the MUCH system :

- the capability to import documents prepared in an SGML-like format into the MUCH representation, and
- the ability to generate traditional documents from the MUCH system

MUCH supports tools for importing textual documents in standard markup languages and builds hypertext where the outline is used as a hierarchical semantic net, and the text under an outline heading is indexed using its heading. The document generation capability is based on a traversal algorithm which performs a extended depth-first traversal of the hypertext document (see Figure 9.14 Traversal System).

Figure 9.13–Create Link: The outline is on the left. Paragraphs that are attached to the nodes appear on the right when the user selects an item from the windows on the left. The user has elected to create another link and is about to enter relevant information in the small, 'pop-up' window in the center of the screen. (Note that links have types).

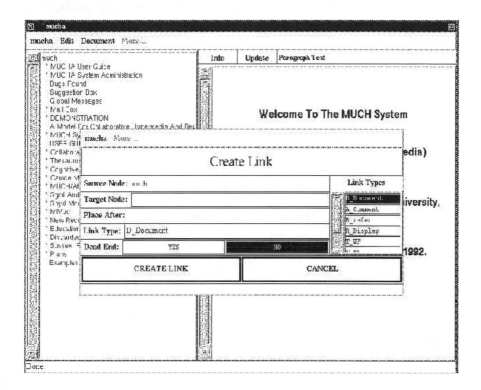

The MUCH system allows a user to take existing documents and create new documents based on these. The user selects a start heading and a level to which a *depth-first traversal* should proceed. New links can be created and certain links may be defined as dead ends so that the traversals can generate documents with significantly different outlines from any currently in the library. The reorganization efforts in MUCH aim at providing different views of the same library according to users' specification. Thus the result in some sense can be seen as a draft of a new document, and users can readily modify the structure and the contents of the draft with the MUCH authoring facilities.

Figure 9.14–Traversal System: Here the MUCH outline system can be seen, and options available to the user for manipulating the outline, are shown. These allow the user to control which of the types of links between nodes that exist in the text should be followed.

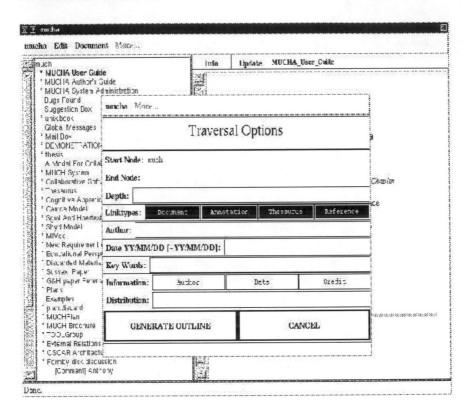

SoftClass

The SoftClass project was funded jointly by Canadian research granting agencies and Tandem Corporation (Mili, 1994). The project aimed to enhance software reuse for distributed management software and priorities hinged upon two alternative goals:

- reuse existing software, and
- to develop object-oriented software.

In SoftClass, the term 'software component' refers to software products at all stages of development, including requirements and design.

Repackaging

One focus of the SoftClass project was the repackaging of documentation. This repackaging relies on:

- a tool called SoftText that uses a theoretical model of technical writing to extract a skeleton software architecture and
- a simple automatic indexer—called SoftIndex—that matches parts of the document to specific vocabularies to support later retrieval.

The representation of software components in SoftClass is similar to Practitioner's questionnaires. Indexing terms belong to predefined (or computable) semantic hierarchies (i.e., taxonomies), and support various retrieval algorithms.

In *SoftClass*, all software component descriptions are instances of description templates or categories (somewhat like the PRESS Questionnaires). In general, for a given development methodology, there is one category for each type of component (e.g., process versus data) and for each level of development. Categories are themselves arranged in a class hierarchy to take advantage of similarities between categories. Each *category* is characterized by:

- a set of relevant attributes and their semantics,
- a set of permissible component categories, and
- a set of permissible generic internal relations.

When defining instances of the category, developers are automatically prompted for mandatory attributes but have to explicitly bring up optional attributes. If an attribute is shared between a component and its sub-components, its values are automatically filled for the subcomponents. If an attribute remains invariant across development stages, its value is automatically filled for subsequent level descriptions. The SoftClass project particularly considered the step from a pre-design or analysis stage to the design stage. For example, the 'purpose' of a software module remains the same at the analysis or the design level. It suffices to specify it for the analysis level.

Alternatives were explored in order that SoftClass's database could be 'populated' with descriptions of existing software components from various sources. The two alternative source were:

textual documentation and
CASE tools export files.

The information contained in these sources is complementary. Textual documentation is destined for human consumption and contains prosaic descriptions that are not found in export files. Export files from CASE tools contain structural information that is missing or hard to extract from textual documentation.

Extracting SoftClass-like descriptions of software components from other CASE tools' export files is fairly simple, and can also be an aid in extracting relevant sections from textual documentation and assigning them the right attributes. However, because of the relatively recent foray of *CASE tools* into software engineering practice, and because most of the early CASE tools offer little beyond drawing capabilities, the project team had to expend considerable effort trying to extract structured descriptions of software components from textual documentation alone. To aid in this they developed the tool SoftText, that extracts a skeleton of software architecture from textual documentation into SQL.

SoftText

Software document outlines reflect:

- the structure of software being documented (decomposition/aggregation and component-attribute relationships),
- the structure of development tasks, and
- various taxonomies (e.g., a taxonomy of attributes and a taxonomy of component categories).

The *extraction algorithm* relies on a categorization of outline headings and a categorization of the relationship between outline headings. With this information, SoftText can reconstruct a skeleton of the software being documented and extract the relevant pieces of text in the core of the document (see Figure 9.15 SoftText Extraction).

Figure 9.15–SoftText Extraction: Analyzing this document and having identified 'Function' as an attribute name, and 'HLQS' as a software component name, SoftText knows that 'Function' is an attribute of 'HLQS,' and that the text immediately following section 1.1 is the textual description of the value 'Function' for HLQS.

1. HLQS System

    1.1 Function

        HLQS provides a high-level interface

When *documentation standards* are closely followed—modulo lexical variations which the tool is able to handle—all section headings and component names can be unambiguously categorized. Additional heuristic rules are used to ascertain the categorization of section headings as component names. Once two hierarchically adjacent section headings have been characterized, there is often only one possible interpretation for the relation between the two.

SoftText takes as input MS-Worddocuments in text format, and produces a file of batch commands (in Smalltalk) to SoftClass to create the extracted components and assign them textual attribute values. SoftText is able to recognize that a component is a subcomponents another of component. However, it does not elicit the exact relationships between them. Such relationships are extracted from export files produced by PowerTools(PowerTools is a CASE tool from Iconix Software Inc.), when they are available, including their graphical layout for the purposes of the graphical interface. In Softclass a simple automatic indexer is implemented that matches textual descriptions to a list of keywords. SoftText complements the extracted information with CASE tools export files, when such files are available.

Transformations

Support for *transforming reusable components* is also embodied in SoftClass. In addition to issues of component classification and retrieval, attempts were made to answer three questions :

1. Given that no component was found that closely matches the requirements, which combination of components (and in what combination) might satisfy them, if any?

2. Given the (partial) description of a desired software component (presented as a query to the software components library) and the closely matching description of a retrieved component, which transformations should be applied to the retrieved component so that it satisfies the desired requirements?

3. Given that a transformation has been applied to a retrieved component at a given development stage (e.g., analysis), which transformation(s) should be applied to its subsequent level descriptions (e.g., design)?

Focus on these problems was motivated by empirical data suggesting that developers are quick to fall back on developing from scratch when a reusable component requires non-trivial modifications (Woodfield *et al*, 1987). The first problem can be seen as a retrieval problem, and provides the basis for bottom-up development. An exact solution to this problem is impractical, if not theoretically impossible, although heuristic methods can be developed that provide potential solutions. The second problem is very difficult to deal with but can be dealt with to some extent. Methods to do this aid in dealing with the third problem.

SoftClass supports *data definition* facilities that promote the reuse of data objects. At the representation level, data objects are treated in the same way as process objects: they have attributes, components, and an internal structure. However, they have one special attribute, 'Operations,' whose value is a list of protocols, each containing a list of related process-like software components that operate on the data object. In SoftClass, the inputs/outputs of process-like objects are represented by attributes. The keyword value of such attributes is the 'type' of the input/output. A process-like component that appears in the 'Operations' of a data object must have that object as a type for one of its inputs/outputs. In addition, data objects support sub-classing whereby a data object inherits both the components and the attributes of its 'super-object.'

At the analysis level, the category Data-Object is used to describe application-dependent data objects, such as 'Customer File,' or 'Product Inventory.' Attributes include things such as 'Update Frequency' and 'Access Authorization.'

At the design level, two categories were defined, one for generic, application-independent data structures, called GenericDataStructure, and one for application-dependent data structures called simply DataStructure. Instances of GenericDataStructure include things such as 'List,' 'OrderedList,' or 'HashTable.' These have generic names for components and operations (e.g., 'GetFirstElement'). A DataStructure is created by mapping a DataObject to a GenericDataStructure. For example, 'Customer File' would be represented at the design level by mapping its analysis level representation to the GenericDataStructure 'HashTable.' The mapping involves:

- mapping the application-meaningful attributes and components of the analysis-level DataObject to the names of attributes and components of the GenericDataObject, and

- mapping analysis-level operations to the operations of the GenericDataStructure.

Part of the latter is done automatically based on the mapping between names of components and attributes. The dual inheritance structure for data objects distinguishes between application semantics and design/implementation semantics, which are traditionally mixed in object-orientation, with adverse effects on the clarity of designs and the reusability of classes. This structure is also referenced by a program design language compiler to validate manipulations on data objects.

SoftClass is a transformational software development tool. Software is developed by starting with more or less formal specifications, leading to some form of program code which is executable, or can be executed. The process of transformation is not completely automatic and the user may be prompted to choose the most applicable transformation at a certain point in the transformation process, if the knowledge SoftClass has is incomplete. SoftClass uses mappings to record development transformations. For those development transformations that can be automated, the mappings are given in a functional format, and when triggered, automatically produce the target descriptions. For those development transformations that require developer intervention, the mapping is recorded after the fact. In either case, a developer is able to predict the effect of local changes at one level of the development process on successive levels. SoftClass implements a trace of the evolution of software through various development phases. The trace is made from a sequence of mappings that echo the transformational process.

Related System

DRACO is another reuse system, like SoftClass,which interacts with and supports the developer during the transformational process (Neighbors, 1989). DRACO is designed to capture and reuse analysis information, rather than lower-level information, such as code modules. A processor accepts high-level descriptions of the desired program and generates the code. Designs for a particular domain are expressed in a formal way, leading to an understanding of the inputs/outputs and processes. DRACO is based upon domains and involves three new human roles in the software development process :

- application domain analyst - a domain expert who can identify common constituents in the requirements of several systems in a domain, or problem area. His or her job is to define the objects and operations important in that domain.

- domain designer - specifies different implementations for these objects and operations in terms of the other domains.

- modelling domain analyst - similar to the application domain analyst but is more concerned with which of these domain requirements have proven themselves general to several areas of interest.

Once the DRACO domain is large enough, new systems can be built from the existing component information. This is software concept level reuse but this can then be transformed into code. The system has many domains, organized hierarchically and some of which contain executable information to allow the transformation of code to take place.

A User Interface Generator

Approaches to reuse may be classified as *compositional* or *generative.* Compositional approaches support the bottom-up development of systems from a library of available lower-level components. Much work has been devoted to classification and retrieval technology and to the development of automated systems to support this. Generative approaches are application domain specific; they adopt a standard domain architecture model and standard interfaces for the components. Their goal is to be able to automatically generate a new system from an appropriate specification of its parameters. The Fourth Generation Languages used in the commercial world can be considered an example of generative reuse. Such approaches can be highly effective in very well understood domains, but significant effort is required to develop the initial model.

Application generators accept specifications of desired application characteristics and generate application products. By example, a generator supporting interactive construction of graphical user interfaces might allow the direct specification of user interface abstractions, such as menus and buttons. An application generator typically manipulates rather high-level constructs and allows the user, in a sense, to readily reorganize the components into a new product. In this sense the *application generator* is a reuse tool. On the other hand, some would argue that an application generator is basically another piece of software and not a reuse tool. The remainder of this section describes a graphical user interface generator and treats it as an example of a reuse tool.

The main overall requirement of a user interface is ease of use. In several ways this can be seen as a subjective thing, though there are several sets of guidelines to help developers. One of the main needs when designing an interface is for consistency (Nielson, 1989). *Consistency* should exist at many levels, from window to window in a program, from program to program on a platform and so on. If all the gadgets (a functional part of the interface, like a button or scroll bar) work in the same way, then the user should be able not only to transfer skills from gadget to gadget, when used for the same thing, (e.g., all scrolling windows have the same sort of scroll bars, whether they scroll text or graphics) but also when faced with a new interface item, will be able to predict what it does by the gadgets it uses. This also reduces potentially costly mistakes which users make. Furthermore, consistency relates to code reuse, as the same code can be used to ensure that all functions of a particular type behave identically.

Figure 9.16–Graphical User Interface Example: This shows the standard Motif file selector.

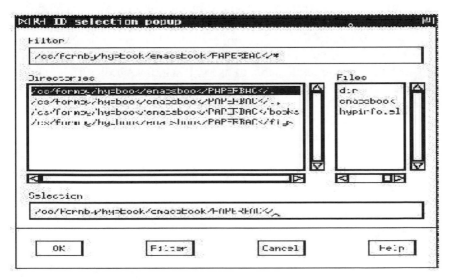

A '*widget*' is a construct used in the building of user interfaces and contains several gadgets. The Motif file selector (see Figure 9.16 Graphical User Interface Example) a compound widget, it is built up from several other widgets, two text widgets ('Filter' & 'Selection'), two scrolled text window widgets ('Directories' & 'Files') and four buttons ('OK,' 'Filter,' 'Cancel' & 'Help'). The code for the text widgets, windows and buttons has been reused to create this widget. If users wish to manually edit the 'Filter' field, they know that they must click on it with the mouse button to type, from their experience with other text widgets. This means documentation for these widgets can also be reused, since the information explaining, for example the action of the scrolled window, can be the same anywhere that a scrolled window is used. The user does still have to learn how the actions of the buttons and clicking on text in the scrolled windows allows them to select a file, but once that knowledge is acquired it is applicable whenever a file is to be loaded or saved with this file selector, in this program or any other Motif complaint program.

The benefits to reusing widgets include less tangible gains. The predictability of the interface gives users a feeling of confidence. If the original interface specification used to design the widgets is well designed and `pretty,' then all consistent interfaces are also likely to be so. Some aspects of consistency are cosmetic, such as fonts and colors, but most are to do with functionality.

Developers are eager to reuse interface widgets not just because of the direct benefits of consistency, but also for other reasons. Developing good user interfaces is a complex and time consuming task. The code for even some of the fundamental objects such as a scrolled window may involve many, many lines of complex code. The benefits of reuse are more obvious, and the ability to reuse is more tangible. Not reusing in a user-interface is often noticeable to users. If windows look different or do not function in the same way as other windows, then users will quickly notice.

Reuse in interface development is made more automatic because of interface development toolkits on the marketplace, for example Microsoft's Visual BASICfor Microsoft Windows, and Hewlett Packard's Interface Architectfor X Window. These are different in many ways but the basic principle is the same in both. The developer creates an interface visually using high level constructs. All code is automatically generated by the package using the specification drawn by the user on the screen and selected from menus. The user writes only code that is domain specific, the rest is generated from reusable templates and code segments by the system.

Interface Architect is a software package by Hewlett Packard for the creation of X Window applications. It allows the user to create interfaces which use the international standard widget set of Motif, with very little, if any actual code having to be written by hand. Interfaces are created by selecting items from menus and drawing on the screen, the interface being drawn as it will look on the screen when completed. Then the user can attach text areas, buttons and so forth to that window by selecting the desired items from menus and dragging out their area. Each of these items can be edited to move them, change fonts, indicate how it behaves when activated, and so on. The developers can add their own code to the various buttons so that when a button is clicked a program is executed. This is in stark contrast to usual methods of creating these interfaces, which involve writing many hundreds of lines of code.

Interface creation is typically complex but unless something specialized or complex is needed a developer can use Architect to create an interface without having to learn anything about the actual physical code needed to perform any task such as opening a window, thus allowing them to concentrate on the actual application-specific segments. Once the interface has been designed, it can be automatically generated. Architect generates stand-alone C code. Developers never need to directly manipulate the generated source code. Instead the constructs can be loaded into Architect and manipulated graphically.

Generic components can be created. It is possible to define parts of the interface, such as the title of a window, using variables. The actual value used at run time (and thus the text that is displayed) is the value of the variables when the call is made to create the window. This feature is described in Hewlett Packard's Architect documentation as a *reusable parametric component*. It means that if similar dialogs are needed for a group of tasks only one need be defined uniquely, the others can be acquired by modifying the values.

As well as creating programs, users can create partial interfaces, thus a developer could create a set of reusable higher level components, which would be of widgets similar in level of functionality to the file selector (which is already predefined) and load them into Architect whenever they are needed. Also Architect provides for reuse by allowing graphical user interfaces to be added to existing command line driven UNIX programs quite simply.

Epilogue

CASE tools support systematic software engineering and facilitate reuse processes. This chapter has emphasized two such tools, namely Practitioner and SoftClass. A user interface generator has also been presented as an example of another kind of reuse tool.

The Practitioner and SoftClass systems emphasize domain analysis. Each helps the user analyze software-related information and encode that analysis into a computerized-representation. Some of the analysis may be automatically done. Retrieval in the Practitioner system is based on word searches, thesaurus searches, or hypertext browsing. SoftClass supports retrieval of software descriptions from queries that are partial descriptions. The authoring of new software or software-related documents is supported by collaborative, hypertext authoring tools in Practitioner and transformational processes in SoftClass.

An application generator is a very different type of reuse tool. Hewlett Packard's Interface Architect is a user interface generator. It has been described in some detail to illustrate the domain model and the assets which application generators need and benefits of consistency and efficiency they allow.

Chapter 10
Case Studies

The major barrier to reuse is often claimed to be managerial or organizational, in the sense of organizing people not organizing information. Accordingly, a study of technological tools for organizing, retrieving, and reorganizing information can only directly address the smaller part of the reuse problem. Managerial models have been introduced in Section 1 of this book but a proper appreciation of those models depends on real world examples or case studies. This chapter presents those case studies. The key issue in this chapter is how companies manage their people in order to achieve software reuse. As part of the Practitioner Project (described in the previous Chapter) work was done at a commercial partner and is also described in this chapter.

Successful Commercial Cases

The following brief sketches illustrate the potential benefits of reuse (GTE, 1992a). The companies tend to be large and several are dealing with military applications. Later in this chapter detailed managerial mechanisms of the corporate giants IBM, HP, and Motorola are presented.

The *Toshiba Fuchu Software Factory* produces software using a standardized life-cycle model. This factory produces process control software products. At Fuchu, the use of metrics has been recognized from the start and reuse has been measured since 1977. A fourteen percent gain in productivity has been achieved annually. `Promote Reuse' is a company motto, and reuse is fully supported by the management. A large library of reusable software items has been developed, and it is standard practice for every project to review possible candidates for reuse at the start and throughout a development project.

The *GTE Asset Management Programme* has been based on a prototype system developed at the University of California at Irvine. This prototype was redeveloped by GTE and resulted in a successful transfer of technology. At GTE, the aim was to support reuse of any asset with the emphasis on software. The production system developed by GTE held over 200 COBOL components. GTE found that in 1987, they achieved a reuse factor of 14% and saved $1.5 million.

Raytheon Missile Systems recognized the redundancy in its business application systems and instituted a reuse program. In an analysis of over 5000 production COBOL programs, three major classes were identified. Templates with standard architectures were designed for each class, and a library of parts developed by modifying existing modules to fit the architectures. Raytheon reports an average of 60% reuse and 50% net productivity increase in new developments.

NEC Software Engineering Laboratory analyzed its business applications and identified 32 logic templates and 130 common algorithms. A reuse library was established to catalogue these templates and components. The library was automated and integrated into NEC's software development environment, which enforces reuse in all stages of development. NEC reports a 7:1 productivity improvement and 3:1 quality improvement.

Bofors Electronics had a requirement to develop command, control, and communications systems for five ship classes. As each ship class was specific to a different country, there were significantly different requirements for each. To benefit from reuse, Bofors developed a single generic architecture and a set of large-scale reusable parts to fit that architecture. Because of a well-structured design, internal reuse, and a transition to modern CASE tools, Bofors experienced a sizeable productivity improvement in the number of lines of code generated per hour.

Universal Defense Systems in Australia develops Ada command and control applications. The company began its work in this business with a reuse focus, and has developed a company-owned library of 400 Ada modules comprising 500 thousands lines of code. With this base, the company developed the Australian Maritime Intelligent Support Terminal with approximately 60% reuse, delivering a 700 thousand line system in 18 months.

Practitioner and the ABB Steel Works

The *Practitioner case study* is concerned with reuse within a Steel Mill control system. Field studies in this domain were done with Peine-Salzgitter Steel Works and Asea Brown Boveri (ABB). ABB implements control systems for steel mills and wanted to establish a work process to improve the quality of software, minimize the risk involved in the production of new software, provide more flexibility when requirements change, and allow the reuse of software components from earlier projects.

The American Association of Iron and Steel Engineers (AISE) has studied the role of software systems in *steel mills*. For steel makers the problems are in general the same as for other software projects, the need to cut costs and maintain quality. The AISE set up a study and identified that reusing software was very desirable in steel mills. Their original aim was for portable programs (ones developed for one system could easily be used on another), but doing this without changing the software was not always possible (Cartwright, 1985). AISE identified the problems with reuse as being :

- no single methodology to support reusability among disparate application areas
- lack of techniques to provide reliable means of storing and retrieving reusable software
- lack of adequate documentation for reusable software, and of means to identify its function
- lack of structuring principles applied in the design of software holding back reuse of functional designs

and with regard to the steel industry

- lack of management commitment for financial and technical support required to develop reusable software
- need for software library development and management
- need for educating software engineers in the steel industry about reuse methods and benefits
- need to impose and enforce reusability guidelines on outside software developers that supply the steel industry.

A big problem when upgrading software in a steel mill control system is that the original system that is to be upgraded was probably written 20 or so years ago and nobody truly knows the old programs in any detail. Also expectations of software now are much greater than they would have been 20 years ago. An example of the life-span of these systems is that at ABB one of the steel mill lines was first made operational in 1963, enhanced in 1975 and again in 1985, this line has always been computer controlled. The Practitioner Project aimed to find a way of reusing at least some of the concepts that this software addressed.

Several studies of steel mills and steel mill processes were analyzed and combined to form a set of concept models or questionnaires to describe processes in the 'Hot Mill Rolling Area' of the steel mill. This formed the *domain analysis* necessary to form a useful model of the steel mill, the processes involved and the materials transformed by these processes. The Practitioner Project built on the results of AISE. Questionnaires were produced to `provide a high level conceptual view' of the control systems in various areas of the plant, for example `Hot Rolling Line Roll Management Systems'. These questionnaires both complemented and augmented existing documentation about the system and planned systems.

Experiments were carried out in-house by the Practitioner Developers and at ABB with the Practitioner tools. Two sets of experiments tested the functionality of PRESSTIGE. In one experiment, a C software package amounting to 2,800 lines of code was redocumented using questionnaires. The entire functionality of the package was documented in questionnaires. Filling the questionnaires took most of the 240 hours spent on the task. Users complained that some aspects of the concept model were either irrelevant or unimportant.

After an introduction into the concepts underlying Practitioner and the tools, two engineers performed tasks related to three major areas:

- thesaurus use and maintenance, using the thesaurus tool,
- locating questionnaires, using the CCL tool and the browse tool, and
- the use of questionnaires for offer preparation in response to an actual call for tenders.

The preparation of a tender for a project was chosen for the purpose of demonstrating the reuse process, as it provides a short illustration of reuse, while at the same time bearing enough resemblance to the design process to make realistic use of the Practitioner methods and tools. The engineers were impressed with the functionality of PRESSTIGE, and especially the browse tool which they felt was a powerful instrument to list relations between objects in the database. However, they felt that

PRESSTIGE lacked tools to navigate directly through questionnaires without going through the thesaurus, suggesting hypertext technology as a natural extension. All participants raised concerns about the tools response time - an implementation detail - but more fundamentally, about the cost of *building questionnaires* for a given application domain.

While ABB was not dissatisfied with the Practitioner tools, ABB has not continued to use the tools. The cost of building a domain model via the Practitioner questionnaires was greater than the benefits which ABB realized. ABB remains committed to encouraging reuse in its world-wide operations but will rely less on new tools and more on managerial innovations.

IBM Reuse

Most major companies have quality management programs. IBM's quality management approach has as a major element the increased reuse of valuable assets such as software, designs, and experiences to prevent redundant development and maintenance efforts. In the late 1980s, IBM launched a *worldwide campaign* to implement reuse formally into the processes of its internal operations.

Significant accomplishments have been made within IBM since the early 1980s in reuse technology. Sites such as Boblingen, Germany, Houston, Texas, and Poughkeepsie, New York have participated in this work. Part of the effort to formalize the management of reuse in IBM can be traced to the work in Boblingen on building blocks. Subsequently the *IBM Corporate Reuse Council* was established. The Council established broad communication channels. These took many forms, including newsletters, a 'starter kit', and electronic bulletin boards (Tiro and Gregorius, 1993).

A focal group called the Reuse Technology Support Center was formed in January 1991. Its responsibility was to coordinate the reuse effort within IBM, provide consulting to technical organizations, and provide funds for tools and assets. In addition, reusable parts technology centers were established. As writing reusable software costs more initially than other software, *management support* is needed to make that investment possible.

The application of reuse at IBM was recognized to occur at different levels. The implementation of reuse in a business area entails exploiting opportunities for software reuse across multiple contracts or products. For project-level reuse the key activity is the establishment of a *project reuse team leader.* The leader participates in all of the project reviews and must be aware of external sources for reusable components.

Implementing reuse for a site requires additional *coordination.* A site champion is given broad coordination responsibilities. A common library of reusable parts is established. The primary focus of the IBM reuse program is to establish reuse across an entire site. Different sites within IBM have taken different approaches to populating their reuse libraries. Some examine their current development efforts and identify and build reuse candidates, while other sites solicit donations.

When the *IBM Reuse Technology Center* was formed, it targeted five sites for support during the first year. By 1993, 30 sites world-wide were involved with the Center. The best programs showed savings in the millions of dollars and reuse accounted for 25 percent of the components in a software product. There have been cases where the finely-tuned data abstractions provided by the building blocks exhibited better performance characteristics than custom-built data structures. These projects have benefited from the reduced maintenance costs as well as the improved performance gains.

Few major breakthroughs are necessary to exploit reuse. Certain attributes of software make software easier to reuse, but these are not necessary for reuse. IBM experience shows that reuse can be accomplished successfully in existing products with *existing techniques and knowledge.*

The IBM Boblingen Experience

At the IBM system software development site in Boblingen, Germany, the first reusable parts center was established in 1987. The objective of the parts center is the production of highly generic reusable software components for worldwide use within IBM (Wasmund, 1993).

Steps

The Bobligen approach followed 5 steps: 1) define the goal, 2) determine critical success factors, 3) define required activities, 4) validate plan, and 5) execute activities. The goal was to establish a well-defined reuse program within two years that would shorten development time, increase reliability of products, and increase the extent of reuse. Brainstorming contributed to the determination of *critical success factors.* The goal was seen to have aspects of trading. In other words, for assets to have multiple applications, it is necessary to establish a trading infrastructure to link customers and suppliers. The elements of a marketplace are derived from the fact that suppliers offer parts and customers require parts.

To store and advertise the parts to be traded, a repository for holding the parts as well as their description is needed. *Traders* must also trust the quality of the parts. As quality is often loosely interpreted, IBM preferred to use the concept of certification level. This means a guaranteed completeness and defect rate of a part. Additionally, the purchaser of a part wants some maintenance assurances. Some kind of accounting is required to record exchanges and associated costs and savings.

Overall, the determination of critical success factors identified the following factors: motivation, education, requirements for parts, offering of parts, part library, quality criteria, maintenance, progress control, and accounting. To increase *motivation*, incentives were introduced as an activity. A part library could initially be a simple list, but communication channels are needed to make known and accessible this library. As the library grows, structured methods and tools to support the library are needed. For certification levels, the lowest was `as-is' for software that was not designed to be reusable but might be of use to someone. The medium level certification indicated a part that can be reused without additional explanation. Maintenance changes to software must be accommodated by the library. *Education* is important at IBM. An appropriate curriculum addressing all aspects of reuse was created.

Validating the Plan

Validating the IBM plan for reuse involves itself several derived activities including:

1. modify development processes,
2. run incentive program,
3. establish communication paths,
4. apply standards,
5. find sources for parts,
6. establish curriculum, and
7. have supporting tools.

In *modifying the development process*, the first modified phase is the requirements phase. As a result of the reuse analysis, the estimated amount of code for a system is divided in the requirements phase into product-unique code and reused code. This separation eventually leads to a list of requirements for parts. This kind of requirement allows for proper subsequent monitoring of progress in reuse. The state of reuse is collected in every development step.

Maintenance effectiveness for reused parts is gained by redefining the appropriate process step such that error reports of customers can be quickly routed to the owner of an erroneous component. More and more products should be composed of building blocks owned by different organizations rather than created new each time. To exploit the economic attributes of reuse, new *accounting methods* are needed. Experiences at IBM shows that there is a lack of progress in determining the value of a reusable part and of availability of flexible charging mechanisms between organizations.

The IBM experience with modifying processes indicates that immature processes are not appropriate to modify. With *maturity* measured on a scale from least mature to most mature, a good starting point for modification of processes so as to better suit reuse was deemed to be a process in the middle of the least to most mature scale. Even at this one can not expect the staff to initially change their day-to-day operations.

The implementation of the process modifications is time-consuming and ideally one would have many years to slowly adapt an organization to a new emphasis. However, the IBM reuse goal was to reach significant results within two years. Accordingly an accelerator was needed. IBM adopted *incentive programs* for reuse. The provider of a reusable part gets credit depending on the size and usage of the part, and the user gets credit for integrating available parts. The award program at IBM Boblingen also is consistent with existing award schemes in its schedule and emphasis on quality, and rewards for usage of unmodified code only. Considering the benefits of reuse, the incentives are a relatively low-cost investment.

The third activity in validating the plan concerns the *communication paths*. Several communication channels were deemed important at IBM, including personal communication, electronic bulletin boards, and databases. Personal communication always proves to be the most important channel when working with representatives of product areas. This person should be recognized as a competent professional and be able to support exchange of information germane to reuse objectives. Bulletin boards are also heavily used for reuse communications.

In the initial phase of reuse, when the repository of parts is small, a simple list of these parts is circulated around the site. Later as the repository grows in size, a database is used. IBM developed a sophisticated database for corporate-wide storage and retrieval of reusable parts for internal use. It is similar to a *literature database*, which is anyhow a reuse database of documented experiences. Searching simple lists for reusable parts works very well for fewer than 500 parts. String search can be easily used to find items in the list. While sophisticated databases are valuable when more than 500 parts are available, the IBM experience shows that even for a large-scale repository that users benefit from the availability of simple lists of available parts.

The fourth reuse activity concerns standards and measurements. Experience shows that covering multiple sites by the same standards requires coordination from a central body. IBM established the Reuse Technology Support Center for this purpose. The most important guideline from this Center says how to measure the number of *reused lines* of code. Financial and productivity calculations can be derived from this measure of number of reused lines of code.

Counting the number of reused lines of code is not always a straightforward process. At IBM, source instructions from a reused part count one, independently of how many times one calls or expands the part (Caruso and Hancock, 1993). The choice of using a subroutine versus a macro should not be made to artificially increase the perceived number of lines of reused code. In one actual example, a project reported 11 thousand lines of reused code. Closer inspection revealed that 5120 line of the 11 thousand came from one macro. The original code contained the 10-line macro and a 'Do' loop: Do i := 1 to 512
MACRO (i).
However to optimize the loop it was unrolled to yield: MACRO (1);
MACRO (2);
...
MACRO (512).
The reuse report therefore contained 512 source instructions and 5120 reused instructions, but does not fairly represent the degree of reuse.

In finding *sources for reuse*, IBM Boblingen had the advantage of multiple existing sources. As previously noted, electronic bulletin boards are a popular medium of exchange about reusable parts. While these bulletin boards have the disadvantages of `as-is' usage without certification of parts, they are attractive to staff. A reusable parts center was also constructed. Finally, as new software is developed it is reviewed by a reuse board for spin-offs that can be contributed to the reusable parts center.

A *curriculum* for helping people understand and employ reuse was designed The concept of reuse was best introduced in the course of transition from third-generation language to object-oriented technologies because object-oriented technologies have many reuse characteristics.

Support tools should be available for reuse. IBM identified three particularly important tool types:

- a repository for reusable parts,
- a source code configuration management tool to support integration of reusable parts into products, and
- a code counting tool to count reused source instructions.

These tools should be integrated. However, presently these tools are not fully integrated, and this lack of integration inhibits the diffusion of reuse.

Figure 10.1–Fingertip Reuse: The figure shows two fingers walking across a book.

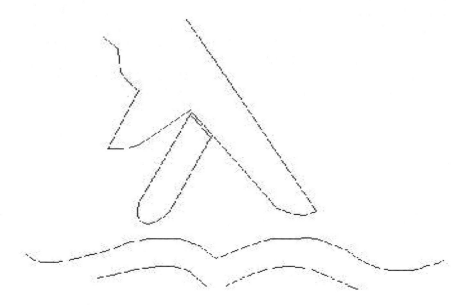

Execution

Two extreme modes of inserting new technologies are the *grass-roots* and the edict approaches. IBM used both. Edicts quickly generate some results. However, experience showed that acceptance by staff of the methodology is not necessarily obtained by the edict approach. Grassroots projects requires patience on behalf of the funding bodies. While incentives are inexpensive, IBM experience showed that only people who already have some affinity to a method will be further motivated by incentives.

The constraints of development organizations to deliver products to market in the shortest possible time does not allow room for additional efforts to produce generalised software. The production of building blocks is therefore the responsibility of *parts centers*. The scope of the parts center may be of various types. At IBM Boblingen the library is of the horizontal type and provides general-purpose building blocks usable in almost any application, such as queues. A vertical type of library was developed and maintained at IBM in Rockville, Maryland. The vertical approach requires that parts be available which are of higher abstraction than needed for the next product release.

At IBM Boblingen the first step in technology transfer was to teach and distribute information about reuse methodology and parts. This step did not actually lead to the application of the new methods. A second step of advice and consultation was added. The decision to get reusable parts for product development happens during the design phase. Therefore consultation was offered to projects in the design phase. This offer was welcomed but not really used. In many projects, design happens very informally and interactively and consultation does not readily fit into this mode of work. Thus IBM introduced a third step, called *fingertip reuse* into the technology transfer process (see Figure 10.1 Fingertip Reuse). Fingertip reuse includes the availability of a tool with which a designer can look for reusable parts within seconds, just when it comes to mind. Otherwise, the threshold of asking for consultation proved too high.

The metaphor of 'let your fingertips do the walking' which has been popularized through advertising for Yellow Pages is appropriate to software reuse. The Yellow Pages are accessible within moments at most offices and homes and users know how to instantly find something which would otherwise be time-consuming to find. As a result of its efforts in reuse, IBM Boblingen was able to triple its reuse rate within 12 months. However, increasing financial and administrative independence of company divisions may lessen opportunities for reuse. The application of the Critical Success Factors method helped the planning and implementing of a reuse strategy, but the execution of the activities required *iterative readjustment*.

An IBM Reusable Parts Center

Prior to the 1980s, reuse of code across project borders at IBM seldom took place. No organizational structures supported cross-project communication, and the lack of a common design language further impeded communication. The code that was written had too many references to global variables.

The IBM Boblingen parts center was started in 1981. In the beginning the goal was to have an integrated software development center that supported the reuse of parts. Investigations into reusable design showed that common structures exist in the areas of data structures and modules. Developers were subsequently encouraged to write software that would allow components to be added to the reuse library. Existing products were scanned to identify replicated functions. A problem of too many *global dependencies* became apparent. Data abstraction became attractive.

In 1983 a project was started to explore data abstraction for a network communication program. Seven abstract data types, called *building blocks*, were written that represented a third of the total lines of code. Due to the good experiences with abstract data types, a reuse model was constructed for it. The model showed the importance of information hiding, modularity, standardization, parameterization, and validation. The programming language PL/S primarily used at IBM at that time was not strong in these features. Therefore a language extension was developed on a second pilot project. The building block language extension BB/LX follows the model of generic packages of Ada.

Building blocks in BB/LX are readily tested. IBM experience has proven the quality gains to be significant. In one project, the quality of the building-block code was about 9 times better than the rest of the code. In another completed, building-block project, no errors were found during the entire test cycle of the product (Bauer, 1993).

As more building blocks were produced, tools for the *library* became more important. Tools for creating, compiling, and testing building blocks were provided. An online library with a catalog aided in selecting the required building blocks.

The expectation that with BB/LX the developers would write their own building blocks was not realized. Instead there was increased demand for building blocks from the *parts center*. A project in 1984 led to a library for which all building blocks have:

- consistent and complete interfaces,
- common terminology, and
- hierarchical implementation.

A comprehensive catalog of reusable abstract data types was provided.

Subsequently, building blocks in C++ were investigated. As C++ was naturally much better suited for reuse than PL/S, the development of the building block library in C++ did not require as much time as for PL/S. In August 1991, the first release of the library for C++ became available within IBM. By the end of 1991, 57 projects with 340 programmers were already using the C++ *building blocks*. Users seem more comfortable with the C++ than the PL/S building blocks. For both languages, few developers use abstract data types as if they were a usual part of the programming language. This makes support in selecting and applying building blocks necessary.

HP Reuse

Hewlett-Packard (HP) has been engaged in software reuse since the early 1980s (Griss, 1993). Early work included the development of libraries of software components written in the BASIC language and more recently the development of libraries in object-oriented programs. Some of these libraries have been widely distributed within HP and some provided to the outside. At the end of the 1980s HP established a corporate-wide reuse strategy. This lead in the early 1990s to the successful application of reuse on a larger scale and the development of further software libraries.

The HP *corporate reuse strategy* involves a core team of software reuse experts with additional people working on assignments with several HP pilot projects. HP is divided into several large divisions, such as the printer division, and unlike some corporations, HP is not building a single corporate-wide reuse library. Rather each division creates reuse programs and products customized to their needs. The core team works with the different divisions to help them exploit reuse. The core team develops economic models, coding guidelines, educational handbooks, and generally consults with the divisions. The core team focuses on domain-specific approaches to software reuse and has developed a domain analysis methodology for HP.

A study of reuse practice at HP has made it strikingly clear that the impediments to improving software reuse are predominantly nontechnical and socioeconomic. When confronted with their first reuse failure, a division should pursue an incremental improvement process. For a reuse program to be effective, the specific inhibitors likely to affect it must be identified. To better visualize these *inhibitors*, HP divides these factors into the following categories:

- people factors include culture, motivation, management, training, and skills,
- process factors include domain, economics, and standards, and
- technology factors include tools and languages.

Once the inhibitors are identified, solutions can be tried.

The most effective reuse programs concentrate on the identification and development of a small, high-quality set of needed, useful components, and make sure that the users of those components know about them. This *small library* of less than 100 components can be handled largely on paper in terms of the catalog and the distribution of information about it. Large libraries of poor-quality components with complex library system interfaces are not wanted. In this way, significant levels of reuse can be achieved in any language with very little tool support. From this base, the reuse effort can grow.

For many kinds of software development, reducing *time-to-market* can be more important than direct cost reduction. Missing a market window can result in a loss of market share. A six-month slip in market introduction in a five-year lifetime product can lose one-third of the potential profit. Under these circumstances, investing in reuse may be the best way to allow subsequent reduction in product development times. For example, one of HP's instrument divisions was able to successfully produce the application software for a new product in less than six months. The division general manager asserted that without their prior investments in reuse which allowed them to achieve 80 percent reuse in their software product, that they would have not been able to meet their time schedule.

For embedded firmware products, recovery from *defects* shipped in the product can be devastating. Increased cost for field service or product exchange can destroy product profits. An estimate based on data gathered at one HP medical division shows that a rework cost due to a firmware error can easily exceed $1 million. HP's peripheral and medical divisions consider reuse as an approach to significantly improve quality and thus a sound investment in reducing long-term costs.

Typical manufacturing organizations expend a significant amount of money to select and qualify vendors and parts. Engineers are then required to design new products using these preferred parts. In one HP software project this *manufacturing approach* to parts acquisition was applied to the design of a real-time database system. The approach resulted in a 25 percent saving in total project cost.

In 1992 HP Laboraties (the research division of HP) initiated a comprehensive, multidisciplinary software reuse program. While the library metaphor has guided much work in software reuse, HP Laboratories is exploring an alternative metaphor to the library. Typically, in the library-centered reuse approach, software code libraries are intended to attract users who have a system design and want a tailorable part. The HP Laboraty metaphor is called domain-specific kits and corresponds to the commercial children's toys from LEGO Systems, Inc., called *LEGO building blocks*. The LEGO metaphor suggests parts that fit together and exhibit ease of use. Over the years, the LEGO Systems building blocks have evolved from a small variety of simple generic parts to a rich family of kits. Kits for spacecraft, for farms, and other domains exist. Each system comes carefully packaged with instructions for how to use it and may sometimes contain frameworks, such as a space platform. The HP Laboraties approach to software reuse exchanges the library metaphor with the domain-specific kit metaphor. The domain-specific kit includes components, frameworks, glue languages, generic applications, tools, environments, and processes (see Figure 10.2 Kit).

Figure 10.2–Kit: In the domain-specific kit, components are placed within a framework and connected with glue.

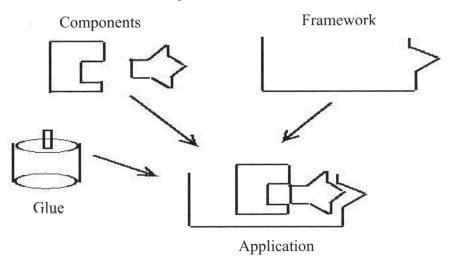

Components   Framework

Glue

Application

HP's HP-VEE system supports the construction of instrument systems and allows engineers to connect virtual instruments together. Components are selected from a palette and assembled using tools and a visual glue language to make complete programs that can then be immediately run. HP Laboraties is exploring numerous *domain-specific reuse kits,* such as a software bus kit. The Laboraties then work with particular divisions to pilot test the utility of these kits.

One way to design a *software factory* based on the kit approach is to consider inputs of user needs and purchased software parts into the factory (see Figure 10.3 Kit Factory). Kit developers than take these two inputs and develop reuse kits from them. Kit users than work with the kits to develop a rich range of software applications.

Figure 10.3–Kit Factory: The two inputs on the left go through kit production and kit use inside the factory before applications result.

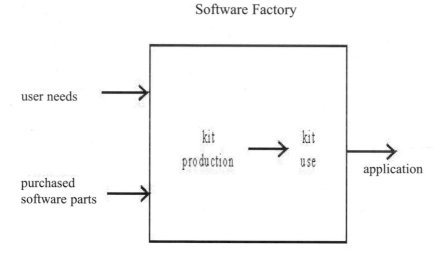

Motorola Reuse

Until the 1990s *Motorola* was primarily a hardware producer. From the beginning of the 1990s the company committed itself to becoming a premier producer of software also. The role of reuse in this multi-year, transitional project can be described as a first-phase, grass roots effort and a second-phase, top-down effort.

Grass Roots Phase

Technical advisors to Motorola recommended that software reuse become a fundamental practice at Motorola. As is often the case in a company considering a new strategy, a *reuse task force* was created. The task force set various guidelines particularly ones on education, motivation, and metrics. Finally the task force was transformed into a reuse working group (Joos, 1994).

Corporate culture at Motorola dictates that major changes be driven from the bottom up rather than the top down. Thus Motorola did not mandate software reuse but wanted the software engineers in the various divisions of the company to drive the software reuse effort. The corporate reuse working group consisted of fifteen engineers who represented the entire Motorola software community. The group concerned itself primarily with *education.* Five person years were invested in offering reuse workshops to the Motorola community.

While the reuse workshops were enthusiastically attended and generated much favorable comment, the net impact of this grass roots approach was negligible. Motorola's middle mangers were reluctant to adopt software reuse because of the up-front costs and slow return on investment.

Top Down Phase

The Chief Executive Officer of Motorola responded to the difficulties of the grass roots approach of the software reuse working group by assigning two senior managers to an indoctrination or top-down effort that includes funded pilot studies. One of the pilot studies was run by top management at Motorola's Israel facility and was based on a *cash incentive scheme.* In one example the reuse of a program saved $15,000 in engineering costs and a bonus of about $1,000 was divided among the engineers involved.

To encourage software engineers to share their software components, the program awards $100 for each approved component that is added to the database of reusable parts. Each time a software component is retrieved from the database for reuse, an additional award is given. This *award* is, at least, 5% of the estimated savings that use of the component brings. The developer receives 40% of the award and the reuser 60%. The Israel group of 150 software engineers has through its cash incentive scheme become the premier example of software reuse at Motorola.

CIM-EXP

CIM-EXP Limited is a typical *small enterprise* consisting of 10 programmer-engineers working on different research and development projects (Kovacs, 1997). Some of the projects are one-of-a-kind to serve specific industrial needs. In these one-of-a-kind projects, any kind of standardization is very hard and complicated.

Other projects employ standards and reuse, but the projects are a challenge to manage due to the specificity of the tool set. Most programming is done in C and C++ and various computer-aided *software engineering* tools are used along with the programming language. The CIM-EXP projects tend to address communication and networking problems, and the design of real-time control systems for flexible manufacturing systems.

One of the approaches to reuse is based on *faceted classification* of reusable components. Reuse is valuable when components can be found that fit into new system needs. The basic approach is to classify part of the design for reuse by strictly using the facets of the classification language to describe all documents and components of the software life cycle. The advantage to this was that the employees developed a certain familiarity with the classification and could use it fairly easily. The problem has been that not all facets apply to all assets. The range of assets that CIM-EXP uses is so wide that the classification system is neither too broad to be useful or so specific that it only partially applies to many assets.

Epilogue

The construction of domain models and libraries that support software reuse has occurred in numerous organizations. The costs of developing and maintaining the libraries are high and only *systematic, reuse-oriented management* of the software staff leads to long-term benefits exceeding cost. This chapter has documented several experiences of software reuse.

At ABB the sophisticated Practitioner tool set and its domain model methodology was not attractive enough for ABB divisions to be willing to further invest in the tool set. The challenge is to *fit into the work flow* of software engineers. For new reuse efforts this fit may require simple tools.

At IBM, *fingertip* reuse has proved critical to user acceptance. If software engineers must consult with the corporate or division reuse librarians in formalized ways, the engineers will not bother to follow the reuse plan. With fingertip reuse, a designer can look for reusable parts within seconds, just when it comes to mind.

The HP experience is consistent with that of ABB and IBM. HP found that the most effective reuse programs concentrate on a small, high-quality set of useful components, and make sure that the engineers know about this small library. At Motorola a cash incentive scheme has proven most helpful to reuse. Again and again the conclusion is that careful focused management of *incremental change* is the key to reuse.

Chapter 11
Courseware Reuse

Courseware is computer-based learning material and a kind of software. Typically the courseware exploits full features of hypermedia. One synonym for hypermedia is interactive multimedia (Rada, 1995). Multimedia contains more than one media. Hypertext is a particular instance of hypermedia which is devoted to textual material, although it may contain photographs, tables, and such.

To what extent can existing courseware be reused to expedite the production of new courseware? For many years courseware authors have tried to determine the factors which influence the efficiency of courseware development. *Reusable, instructional templates* within authoring tools were identified as contributing to efficient courseware authoring over 15 years ago (Avner, 1979). As the availability of multimedia courseware components has increased, the attractiveness of building and exploiting *libraries* of this material has grown. Several large international projects have recently focused on developing tools for such libraries (Chen and Rada, 1994) and on populating such libraries (Margiotta and Picco, 1993).

Despite the reduction in cost of hardware and improved functionality of authoring software, the development effort required to produce hypermedia courseware is still substantial. In the aerospace training sector, one company spends about 400 hours in developing each hour of training material. The inclusion of high quality sound, animation, or video can mean that developing a course from which students gain 1 hour of training time will require 800 hours from the authors of the courseware. Developing courseware is *very expensive*.

The main methods for estimating hypermedia courseware development include educated guesses, industry averages, and formulas

201

(Marshall *et al*, 1994). Educated guesses have proven particularly unreliable. Industry averages vary widely from circumstance to circumstance. The *Cost Estimating Algorithm for Courseware* (CEAC) uses a composite model to estimate both courseware development time and cost (Barnes, 1992). The model uses both course-independent and course-dependent parameters. For instance, course-independent parameters include 'overhead rates' and 'labor rates.' Course-dependent parameters include 'instructional sophistication' and 'availability of existing lecture material.'

Libraries of media are being made available for reuse in various projects. For instance, the University of Bristol has produced a videodisc with 36,000 biomedical images. Copyright of the images remains with the donors of the images. The images can, however, be freely reused for teaching and learning purposes within educational establishments for non-profit making purposes. A catalogue of the material is available and can be searched electronically (Williams and Hammond, 1994).

In a film, the production cost of a single frame often costs over $300. Amazingly this ultraexpensive footage is only used once. Experience has suggested that the probability of finding and buying the right image(s) to fit into a movie is so low that producers would rather make their own footage from scratch. Several efforts have been made to build *video libraries* which could be reused. The MIT Media Laboratory experimented with repurposing footage from the soap opera Dallas for interactive replay. The experiment failed because this apparently multithreaded soap opera was too tightly structured to be repurposed. The Laboratory is now exploring new tools to support video reuse (Goldman-Segall, 1993).

This chapter will first describe standards for courseware that are intended to support reuse. Then two systems that support courseware reuse are presented. One was developed for a small company, the other, for a large company. The features are widely different, as one might expect. Finally, large libraries of educational software modules are introduced.

Courseware Standards

Courseware components can be reused when appropriately classified and embedded within environments that have standard interfaces. *Standards* have been developed by the aviation industry that standardize what these components should be like so that such reuse can be facilitated.

The aviation standards for courseware recommend guidelines for the interchange of the elements that occur in courseware. These elements include:

- Text,
- Graphics,
- Video,
- Audio, and
- Logic.

The standard recommends the use of authoring systems able to export and import courseware elements in standard formats. Specifically, the authoring system must be able to:

- Export and import all basic elements to individual files in standard industry formats.
- Export and import lesson logic to a text representation.

The *recommended formats* for courseware elements emphasize the common ones. Logic elements can be stored in one or more plain text files per lesson. The text files may contain programming language code, a scripting language, or standard generalized markup language-tagged text. The content, in whatever format, must be comprehensive and clear enough to enable a person with a good understanding (of the scripting or markup language) to reproduce (without any other information) the exported courseware completely.

Files can be used to describe a course's content and structure. The level of complexity determines the number of files required and the amount of information required in each file. The following list briefly describes the contents or purpose of several of the files:

- *Course Description File*: Information about the course as a whole including a textual description of the course, and general makeup of the course—the number and type of elements.
- *Course Structure File*: The basic data on the structure of the course, including how the elements are organized.
- *Objectives Relationships File*: Objectives have complex and variable relationships to other elements of a course. This file defines all of these relationships.

Files are the most common data structure in computer science and by asking that the courseware structure be represented in files, the standards developers have reached to the lowest common denominator among the target audience, as standards developers are expected to do.

In the past, authoring systems made the courseware author and student user a captive of the authoring system vendor. If the customer wanted to manage a set of students in a class, he had two choices:

- Design his own management system with his authoring system tools, or

- Purchase a management system from the same vendor who supplied the authoring system.

In either case, the management system works only for course content from a single vendor. This is fine, until the customer acquires course material prepared with a different authoring system. Standards should promote interoperatibilty (AICC, 1997). Interoperability means the ability of a given management system to handle lessons from different origins. It also means the ability for a given lesson to exchange data with different management systems.

There are two ways to enable interoperability of management with lesson delivery:

1. *Lesson launch*: The management should have a standard approach to lesson initiation.

2. *Communication*: The management should have a standard approach to providing information to the lessons and receiving information from the lessons.

Interoperability works as follows:

- The management system creates a file containing the data necessary to start-up a lesson.

- Once the lesson is initiated, it reads the data file created by the management system.

- The lesson system must create a file containing data to be passed back to the management system so that the management system can update its student performance data and make the next assignment.

- When the student leaves the lesson, the lesson system updates and completes the file of information for the management system.

- The management system reads the lesson-to-management file, updates applicable student data, and determines the next student assignment or routing activity.

Management system and lesson system communication is two-way. The *management system* sends information to the lesson when it begins. The lesson sends information to the management system when the lesson ends.

A standard for the virtual classroom concerns the management of the students in the classroom. The standard describes how a *student's performance* should be tracked. This tracking information must be possible to extract from the virtual classroom system that collects it. The models of intelligent tutoring include a student model, a pedagogy model, and a domain model. The student performance information could be seen as part of the student model, but now collected by the teacher to manage a classroom of students.

Rather sophisticated courseware systems have been developed that purport to support reusability of courseware components. These would include, for instance, the LearningWorks systems. LearningWorks (Goldberg *et al*, 1997) allows students and teachers to visualize complex relationships among concepts and software components and to directly author new modules by building on existing modules. The system is based on SmallTalk and evidently works well for developing courses about SmallTalk and for students learning Smalltalk. How well it would generalize to handling general-purpose educational needs is less clear.

Small Company

Integrated Radiological Services Limited (IRS Ltd) is a small company with seventeen employees that specializes in diagnostic radiology and authors courseware about radiological safety. IRS Ltd has a large number of potential reusable components around the office, the majority of which are not currently being used by courseware developers at IRS Ltd. IRS Ltd develops its courseware with an authoring package called Toolbook from Asymmetrix Corporation and decided to develop facilities in Toolbook to support courseware reuse.

Figure 11.1–Entry: This screen from the IRS Ltd system shows the 'Table of Contents' and 'Media Index' options which the user first faces.

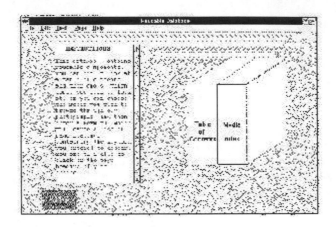

System Architecture

The IRS Ltd system supports librarians in entering material into the library and authors in accessing material from the library. The authors at IRS Ltd identified eight types of material that they wanted the library to contain:

- Text
- Diagrams
- Photographs
- Graphs
- Tables
- References
- Questions/Answers
- Programs

and considered each type of material to be a distinct media type. The material is organized in the library according to *media type* and to domain type (see Figure 11.1 Entry). Each reusable component within the database is of one of the eight media types previously listed. Furthermore, each component has a textual description associated with it. This courseware library also possesses a table of contents which incorporates the main topics within the field of diagnostic radiology from the table of contents of a book of diagnostic radiology. Each heading in the table of contents may correspond to many reusable components of different media types.

In developing and maintaining the library several different roles must be fulfilled, including that of Collector, Populator, and Indexer. The *Collector* takes a list of items from the author, finds the actual items, and gives them to the Populator. The *Populator* converts the material into a format which is compatible with the courseware library and then enters the reusable components into the courseware library. The *Indexer* is required to place a text caption with each component that describes the key concepts conveyed by the component. The Indexer also maintains the Table of Contents and the list of Media Types. The scenario for retrieval from the courseware library begins when the author selects the type of access to the library, i.e., table of contents or media index. On selecting the media index, the author next selects the type of medium he wishes to examine. Then he enters keyword(s) which describe the topic on which he wishes to retrieve components. The computer next searches the components of that media type within the library. If the author selects 'photograph' from the media index and then enters the keyword 'burn,' a photograph of a burn may be retrieved (see Figure 11.2 Typical Screen of the Reusable Courseware Library). Authors are also able to retrieve relevant material from the library by selecting a heading from the table of contents.

Multiple instances of *Toolbook* windows can be on the screen simultaneously. The author uses one instance of a Toolbook window in retrieving components from the library and another instance of a Toolbook window in directly creating the new course. Material to be reused is transferred from the reusable courseware library to the courseware being developed by the author.

Development versus Exploitation

An exercise was performed to ascertain whether the addition of materials to the library followed by the development of courseware using the material within the library helps to reduce authoring costs. Material which is not in a format compatible with the courseware library is first *converted* into an appropriate format. Text presents itself in a wide variety of formats. Text which is to be reused from documents only available in paper form may be processed by scanning the text into the computer and using optical character recognition software. Toolbook possesses an 'import' facility which allows plain text to be automatically imported. Figures which are paper-based are also first scanned. For the purposes of this courseware library, all figures were converted to a bitmap format and then imported into the library. The populators found the scaling of the images more time consuming than other tasks, as this often involved trial and error.

Figure 11.2–Typical Screen of the Reusable Courseware Library: Image showing the facilities available during retrieval of a media type to visit other components of the same type. The photograph presented in the right half of the computer screen shows fingers with radiation burns.

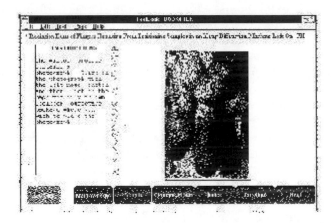

After the library is ready, the *author* uses the material within the library to author courseware. The time taken for the author to do this task is noted. Hence, the time taken for the author to develop courseware with the aid of the tool can be calculated and this can be compared with the time taken for the author to develop a similar piece of courseware without the aid of the tool. The values obtained are substituted into the following relationship:

$$T_{A \text{ with Library}} M_A + T_C M_C + T_P M_P + T_I M_I ? T_{A \text{ alone}} M_A \text{ where}$$

- $T_{A \text{ with Library}}$ is the time taken by the author to develop courseware with the aid of the course library in hours;

- M_A is the wage paid to the author per hours;
- T_C is the time for the Collecting of material for the Library (P for Populator and I for Indexer).
- M_C is the hourly wage paid to the Collector; and
- $T_{A\ Alone}$ is the time taken by the author to develop the course-ware without the aid of the tool.

At IRS Ltd, the librarian-skilled staff are paid $7 per hour, while the authors, who are also domain experts, are paid $15 per hour. For the single course developed in this exercise, the cost of the author's time is about $80 and the librarian costs are about $500. Developing the course by the author alone costs $240. How many courses of similar size to the one already developed and such that all components come from the reuse library would have to be developed before the cost of the library was less than the *benefit of the library*? The inequality given earlier of

$$T_{A\ with\ Library}\ M_A + T_C\ M_C + T_P\ M_P + T_I\ M_I\ ?\ T_{A\ alone}\ M_A$$

would be 'greater than' for 1 or 2 courses but 'less than' for 3 or courses.

The cost of developing the library should include the cost of developing or acquiring the software for the library. The library software was developed by one software engineer working with one radiologist at an approximate labor cost of $5000, which is much greater than the cost of collecting, populating, and indexing the small amount of material which this library holds. If this cost of software is added to the previous equation, the new equation is

$$T_{A\ with\ Library}M_A + Software + T_C M_C + T_P\ M_P + T_I\ M_I\ ?\ T_{A\ alone}\ M_A$$

For this inequality about 40 courses must be written from the library before the library proves *cost effective*.

Media Index versus Table of Contents

The Table of Contents was a useful guide for text retrieval (Rada, 1996). Unexpected problems occurred when the author tried to use the *table of contents* within the reusable courseware library to retrieve material other than text, for example, diagrams or photographs. If there was a section within the book called Introduction, then this would suggest that the text in this section of the book was introductory. If however, a diagram, graph, photograph or table was included in this introductory section of the book, the author could not anticipate the content of the media. The author was unable to develop courseware using the table of contents alone because he was only able to effectively retrieve text from the library, and the courseware which the author wished to develop was multimedia.

The author found the *media index* easier to use than the table of contents in some ways. The author was able to first decide the medium he wished to examine and then enter a keyword describing the topic on which he wished to retrieve material. However, the author was not practically able to develop courseware using the media index alone, because he could not get an adequate overview simply by accessing the media index of what was available within the courseware library.

Results show that neither the media index nor the table of contents alone are enough to support good recall or precision but together the media index and table of contents do support *effective retrieval* (Acquah, 1994). The author found the table of contents index useful as he was able to see, from the headings in the contents window, what was present within the library. This enabled the author to access easily the text he required and also helped him to decide on relevant keywords to enter when using the media index to retrieve text. The author spent the majority of his time retrieving material using the media index, but used the table of contents index when he wished to orientate himself. To improve the speed with which items could be retrieved from the library and thus increase authoring speed, both the table of contents and the media index should be present.

Collecting material which might go into a courseware reuse library is a major task. At some juncture, this material must be assessed for its true value to the library and such assessments are themselves difficult. Getting the material into the proper format for the library is a job for multimedia which is more complicated than for text. Digitising video, for instance, requires powerful hardware. Indexing the material for the library is another major activity. While some indexing can be done automatically, much experience suggests that human indexing, while laborious, is important.

With these various costs to acquiring and evaluating material for the library the challenge of building a large enough library to be useful is clearly daunting. Furthermore, the contents of the library must be continually updated and this must be done in close communication with the needs of the users of the library. In the fast evolving world of hypermedia, new formats themselves are regularly introduced and old ones made extinct. Maintaining the *format converters* for this multimedia library is a technical problem and in a sense easier to handle than the complex problems of content and user satisfaction, but is nevertheless a significant problem.

The Toolbook authoring package used for the development of the IRS Ltd tool was not designed to facilitate the building of courseware libraries or to act as a database. When building libraries for reusable courseware components, a standard database should be used to store the artifacts so that searches can be done quickly and easily. This technical problem was addressed with the next system to be discussed. More importantly, the next system explicitly supports collaborative work.

Coordination

The experiences with IRS Ltd system have indicated various important features of courseware reuse libraries. The conceptual model for the library and the mechanisms for supporting coordination can be extended. One project for the training division of a large, Italian, aerospace manufacturing company, called Augusta SpA, has produced a particularly sophisticated prototype courseware reuse system. The overall system is called *Open System for Collaborative Authoring and Reuse* of courseware (OSCAR).

Reuse Architecture

The OSCAR architecture represents the way in which the OSCAR services are organized, what functional level they realize, and what relationship exists between them. To better represent the organization of services provided by OSCAR and the relationship between them, *OSCAR services* have been grouped in layers (see Figure 11.3 The OSCAR Layers). OSCAR provides the following layers:

- Hardware Platforms: contains all hardware components supported by OSCAR;
- Operating Systems: contains the operating systems supported by OSCAR on the various hardware platforms;
- Communication Space: provides services supporting the distribution of the system and the network management;
- Common Information Space: supplies information management services relevant to the library;
- Coordination and Reuse Space: this layer provides high level services to support coordination and reuse for a courseware library.

Figure 11.3–The OSCAR Layers: Four layers are depicted here. OODBMS means object-oriented database management system.

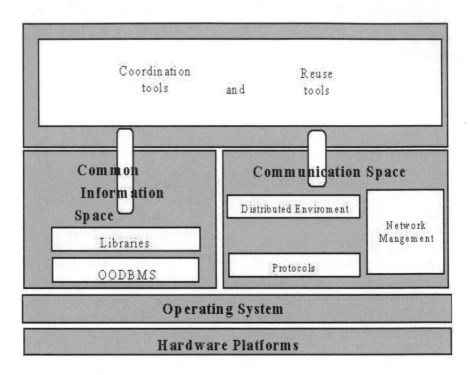

Client workstations represent the user entry point into the OSCAR system. The OSCAR client workstations are mainly multimedia personal computers on which library applications run. They also allow access to shared services such as email, file transfer, and information management. They can be remotely connected to allow a distant author to get access to the OSCAR services. The OSCAR server provides multi-user services in the distributed environment. Operating system services provide the management of all physical resources of a computer system and establish the basic execution environment for applications. UNIX serves as the multi-user operating system. MS-WINDOWS is the reference operating system for the client workstation.

The OSCAR *Common Information Space* (CIS) allows different software components and different users of the system to share information, update them consistently, and base their work on the work of others. The

CIS includes instructional objects each of which has an 'instructional component' and a 'presentational component.' The objects of the Instructional Component (see Figure 11.4 Two Components of CIS) include domain objects which are produced by a Domain Analysis and Student Modeling objects. On the other hand, the Presentational Component includes the physical representation of the actual learning material. The MultiMedia Unit (MMU) is a composition in space and time of several Monomedia Units (MUs). Examples of MMUs are pictures with captions, but also couples or triples of pictures, pictures with voice, and so on. A single picture, a text, or a sound sequence are examples of MUs (see Figure Screen onto Media Units). Of course, there is a need for an object that specifies how several MUs can be combined in space and time to make a MMU. Such an object should also be able to handle small interactions among MUs and diversified exits from a MMU. This object is called 'layout,' and it has been defined as a separate object to allow an author to present the same MMU in different ways, and various MMUs in the same way.

The CIS includes a *pedagogical classification schema*. This pedagogical classification schema functions as a kind of domain-specific filter between users and the CIS (Persico *et al*, 1992). A MMU may be characterized by the pedagogical classification schema in terms of attributes, such as student background, teaching technique, and domain. A flexible and powerful description and classification schema is necessary for the purpose of efficient retrieval and reuse of MMUs.

The *Reuse Services* support both the retrievability and the customization of training material. The functionalities offered by the Reuse Services include conversion tools to reuse material originally available in a format different from the desired one. With the conversion facility, the user who is examining a particular monomedia unit may convert that unit into any of many different formats (see Figure 11.5 Converter).

Coordination Services

The coordination services manage the interdependencies between activities performed by multiple actors. Components of the Coordination Service (see Figure 11.7 AME components) include:

- *Activities* are sets of tasks for achieving a goal.
- *Roles* specify the responsibilities and duties of people.
- *Workspaces* contain resources associated with roles.

Figure 11.4–Two Components of CIS: MMU is multimedia unit.

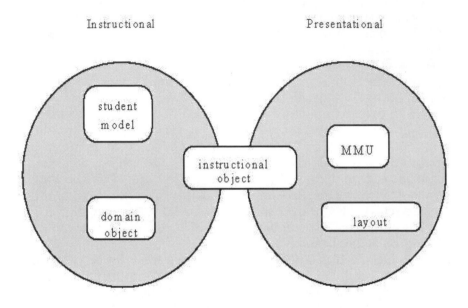

Figure 11.5–Screen onto Media Units: This screen dump from the OSCAR system shows some of the features of the CIS, particularly media units.

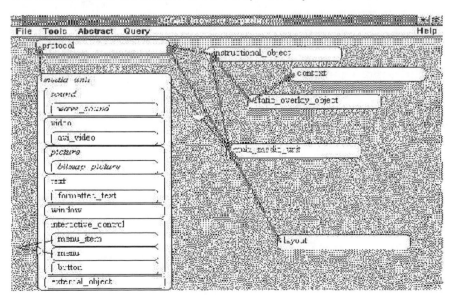

Figure 11.6–Converter: Screen dump from the OSCAR system which presents information about a particular image or bitmap and gives the user an option to convert that bitmap into a variety of formats.

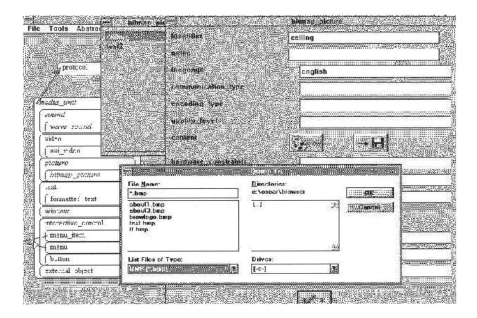

- *Messages* are objects that flow between the role instances associated with an activity.
- *Information Units* are used in building messages.
- *Rules* constrain the behavior of components.

Roles, people, workspaces, information units and messages are represented as objects and are stored in the Organizational Manual. In OSCAR the Organizational Manual and other information germane to coordination are stored in the CIS.

For the development and maintenance of the courseware reuse library, OSCAR defines several roles and activities. Prominent roles include collector, selector, populator, indexer, indexing language expert, and quality assurer. First material for the library must be collected by the 'collector.' Then a 'selector' decides what of the collected material is of appropriate quality to go into the library (Rada *et al*, 1987).

Figure 11.7–AME Components: The relationships among roles, message, activities, and other components of AME are indicated here.

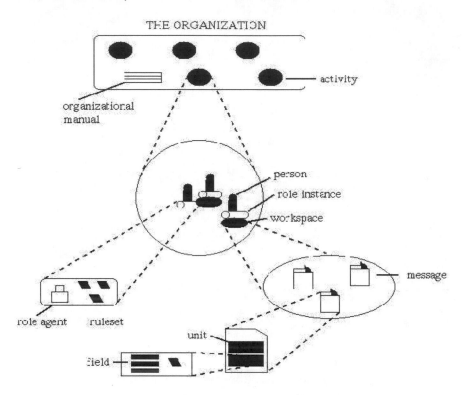

The populator prepares the material for entry into the library and physically enters it. This may involve scanning material or converting formats. The indexers assign index terms to the library. Simultaneously, the indexers work with the indexing language experts to create an indexing language. As the library and its index grows, maintaining the indexing language becomes itself a job (Mili and Rada, 1988). The quality assurer does quality control and specialists on quality are needed to correspond with every other role just mentioned.

For the *Coordination Services* all intermediate products can be treated as messages. For example, when an indexer proposes changes to an indexing language expert, a message is created in the indexer workspace using a template from the organizational manual. The message records information about the person who created it, the role the creator was playing, and the time it was created. The indexer completes the message.

The *workspace* tries to determine which person should deal with the message next based on attributes of the message. In this case the workspace forwards the message to the indexing language expert workspace and tells the indexing language expert role that a message is awaiting attention. If the message can be processed, the role instance locks it until the process finishes.

The indexing language expert workspace retrieves an 'assessment of proposal' template from the organizational manual. By default, the person performing the role would fill-in the details in the appropriate information unit of the message. However, some of the fields within the *information unit* in the message may be filled-in automatically by the role agent. After the person or the role agent fills-in the fields, the workspace unlocks the message and informs the current information unit that it is complete. At this stage, the information unit triggers its rules which check the validity of the field values and determines which will be the new current unit and which role will process it. The message then routes itself to the appropriate workspace.

This circuit is repeated until all the information units are completed. At this point the message is considered complete and the next message is activated and routed to the appropriate workspace. In this way, *indexing language maintenance* is supported by the computer.

The preceding sketch of indexing language maintenance is only a small part of library maintenance. The 'reuse assurance role' monitors the extent to which authors are using the library. A search librarian helps the author find material. In the OSCAR scenario, searching and browsing the CIS is supported by computer programs, but experience suggests that human assistance would also be important.

Educational Object Economies

In addition to the aviation industry, other organizations are concerned about the standardization of educational technology. Educom is an association of higher education institutions that tries to improve the use of technology in education. Educom has produced a standard called the Instructional Management Systems (IMS) *Metadata Specification* (Educom, 1997). This specification is directed toward describing learning resources that are accessible, or perhaps just catalogued, online. The IMS Metadata Specification consists of three primary parts: a dictionary of terms, a description of learning resource types, and a system for managing the Specification. The IMS Dictionary identifies the terms that constitute IMS Metadata. These are the terms that are used to label the learning resources. IMS Metadata is broken down into fields and corresponding values. All of the proposed available fields are defined in the dictionary and their values are enumerated. These fields include author, credits, interactivity level, learning level, objectives, platform, prerequisites, price code, user rights, and user support. The hope of Educom is that all higher education institutions will use this metadata format to characterize their online educational material. Educom is working with the World Wide Web Consortium in the introduction of metadata information into the specification of the World Wide Web itself so that this metadata standard is conformant with other efforts at standardizing metadata formats across all web content.

This interest in obtaining wide usage of components across the web is echoed by other organizations in various ways. For instance, Apple Corporation has led the way in organizing an *Educational Objects Economy* (EOE). This library of reusable objects could be indexed with the IMS Metadata format to increase the accessibility of the information to various communities.

An EOE is a community of people working together to improve the quality and availability of web-based learning materials. Apple, NSF, universities, publishers, and many others have created a first exemplar EOE (EOE, 1997) in June 1997. A key part of an EOE is web site technology that helps empower community members to work together. An EOE web site must allow members to easily gather, share, and add value to *web-based materials* of interest to the community. The technology required to set up an EOE is relatively straightforward. However, creating a vibrant community that is actively achieving its goals, and reflecting that activity through the web site, is a challenging task.

Fundamentally an EOE is a *community of communities*; that is, a community of educators (and learners), developers, and businesses, focused on the creation and collaboration of educational activities which include pieces of Java software in them. The EOE is funded by a joint National Science Foundation and Defense Advanced Research Projects Administration grant.

The History of EOE

Apple has researched a number of authoring tools but realized that no matter how good or easy-to-use an authoring tool is, any authoring tool will only address a certain percentage of the population. Not everyone is interested in learning to use these tools. Further, while authoring tools can empower individuals to create *educational objects*, they do not help an author answer the question "does what I want to create already exist?" Because of this, duplication of effort is common.

To address the issues of duplication of effort, lack of organization, and the (relatively) small authoring community, an on-line community and searchable resources are needed. From a developer's perspective, the EOE can help creators of Java educational applets know what has already been created and by whom. The EOE is also intended to help educators and learners access this material and the creators of the *Java applets*. Working together, the educators, learners, and developers can collaborate to enhance existing material and produce new innovations. The EOE vision relies on a strong, diverse community of users and creators who form small partnerships to modify something that exists or create something completely new.

After four months of operation, the EOE had a library of over 1,000 pointers to Java applets, over 25% of which made source code available. In addition, about 100 people had signed up to be members of the community. The organizers of EOE believe that over time a whole class of domain-specific education communities will start to develop around repositories and directories. Accordingly, the EOE have made the *infrastructure* available for download for anyone who'd like to use it to start their own EOE.

EOE Plans

The EOE started as a directory of freely available resources on the web with a community of people who are willing to work together to share and add value to these resources. Nevertheless, long-term EOE encourages the development of EOE-related businesses and for-profits. Just as libraries do not put bookstores out of business, but spur demand for books through a more literate population, the EOE of free resources should expand the market for "for-fee" educational resources. For example, teachers who start using the EOE would to be able to know which EOE objects are associate with chapters in the textbooks that they are using in their classes. So publishers might provide indices from their textbooks to be freely available, and for fee web resources that could be augments to the printed textbook. Meta-data and micropayment systems are part of the infrastructure that is being developed to support these sorts of businesses.

The EOE has worked with developers to produce different types of license agreements for sharing source code. For example, if a developer wants to use objects from the EOE (perhaps developed at a university) and incorporate those into a product, a certain license would best meet the needs of the developer and the university creator of the original educational objects. The type of license is called an *intellectual capital appreciation license* and allows source code to be shared, as long as bug fixes and ports of the original code are shared back with the community.

Epilogue

Courseware is a kind of software and *courseware reuse problems* are a particular case of software reuse problems. This chapter has examined two courseware reuse tools and experience with their use. As was the case for software reuse at IBM, HP, and Motorola, one general impression is that the tools might be simple to fit into the workflow for initial courseware reuse efforts.

A model of courseware development via reuse from a courseware library has been elaborated. This model has been contrasted to a model of courseware development without reuse. A major challenge for courseware reuse which is not confronted for software reuse in general concerns the wide variety of incompatible *media formats*. The challenges of converting courseware components from one format to another have been largely overcome through the provision of various conversion tools. The conceptual overview of the library contents has been divided into two high-level types, namely a media view and a contents view. Neither alone supports adequate retrieval but both together do.

If a courseware library is developed and is only used by one author to develop one piece of courseware, then the *efficiency* of the reuse process will be very low. A reusable courseware library is most efficient when it is used to develop numerous courses. As the costs of developing and maintaining a multimedia courseware library are relatively high, a small firm might best choose a simple facility and try to quickly realize some benefit from the system. Larger firms may be able to afford larger start-up investments in the library. The critical factor in cost efficiency is a repeated use of the library which will depend in part on the firm's management policy.

Chapter 12
Conclusion

Software reuse is an important aspect of controlling and reducing software costs and improving quality. Successful reuse depends on both managerial and engineering concerns. The *engineering concerns* are with the representation of software assets and their manipulation. The managerial concerns are with the plans of an institution and with its handling of its human resources. The costs and benefits of reuse are multitudinous. Nevertheless currently reusability, when it takes place is usually the result of informal methods and chance rather than a powerful driving force behind software development. A reusability driven development methodology should be utilized for software, so that existing projects both reuse existing components and create new components to be reused in future projects.

The engineering of assets can be viewed from multiple *perspectives*. In one view assets are created, managed, and utilized. In another view, assets are organized, retrieved, and reorganized (see Figure 12.1 Principles of Reuse). In any case, these perspectives must account for both the activities of people and of assets.

Representations

Traditionally reuse focuses on the reuse of code only. This requires least effort from the developer and offers the most immediate returns, when successful. It also has its roots in the component libraries associated with languages like Fortran, or in systems such as X Windows with its widget code that implements buttons and windows and is easily accepted by developers. The code is pre-written, pre-documented and pre-tested.

221

However more than code can and should be reused, if full reuse is to be achieved. All information produced during the *software life-cycle* should be reusable to some extent and tools should be available to the developer to help him or her in the reuse of this information. Typically, the knowledge used and produced at the earlier development stages of software tends to be expressed and presented in a human or human manipulable language, while in the later stages of the development process representations are closer to, or actually are, computer languages. Neither form is problem-free for reuse.

Often the software library will not have a suitable component (code is very specific). Developers may find the component difficult to understand. Any changes other than very minor ones may involve reverse-engineering the component to reach a state where it can be reliably modified. Often the testing advantage is lost, since the component has to be modified or is being used in an environment different enough from its development domain to warrant retesting.

Industry View

The increased size of the global market increases the potential for the number of units to be sold. This permits a business to justify increased capital investment in a product while lowering per-unit price, if penetration of a large percentage of the now larger potential market can be ensured. Penetration, though, is crucially linked to being first to the market. Software developers, therefore, find themselves in a situation of coping with the commodity pricing of high-capitalization software with market share strongly linked to the speed of introduction. This trend is favorable to software reuse because reuse practices support the economical *capitalization* of development effort in a manner that can accelerate the introduction of new products to the market.

Experience in software development has frequently shown that the challenge to software reuse is less the development of new programming languages or technologies, but rather the way an organization *rewards software reuse* on the part of its software engineers. Motorola software engineers in one division were given financial rewards for storing assets in a library and then given significant further rewards each time the asset was used in another product. Those incentives helped that division become the premier example of software reuse in Motorola.

Figure 12.1–Principles of Reuse: The software reuse-cycle. Reusable components are added to the library system, the `organization' being performed by an indexer. On the formulation of queries the system retrieves components and presents them back to the developer. The developer then modifies or reorganizes these retrieved components, perhaps retrieving further components if needs change and adding new material to create a new product.

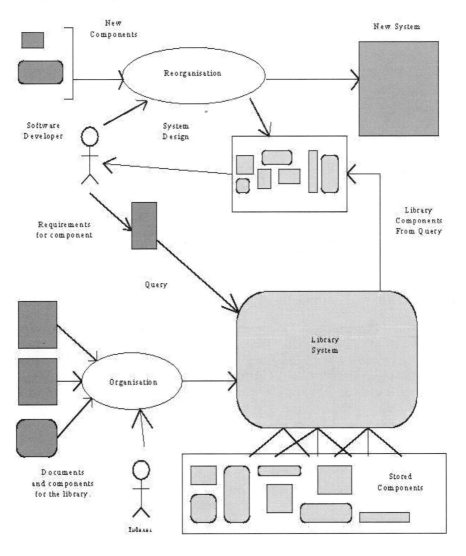

Projects at *IBM* have involved various sophisticated object-oriented approaches to creating assets, but one of the most potent conclusions of the IBM experiences was that tools and methods should integrate seamlessly into the work environment. The greatest impact on reuse came when IBM software engineers could have the reuse library at their fingertips—they could easily move between relevant library contents and the problem solving for which reuse was relevant.

The mere presence of a usable *library* is sometimes "good enough" and additional investment in cataloguing mechanisms and search tools may provide little payback. This argues for purchasing a library tool or outsourcing a reuse library service and focusing one's own investment on the contents of the library rather than the nature of the tool.

There is another side to the industry reuse story. Customers, not just a company's own software teams, may want to have access to reusable software libraries. In the *World Wide Web* market, Microsoft, Netscape, and others are trying to gain market share with customers who want to gain access to reusable code libraries for building interactive web sites. Having components in standardized languages that can interpolate in standard ways with various web-related functionalities is important to such reuse libraries. So some of these software houses feel compelled to compete in being able to label their products as standard in a way that befits the generation of customer-accessible reuse libraries.

Government View

Companies often see their approach to internal software reuse standards as important to their competitive advantage. Some of these companies will keep these software reuse standards confidential. Government agencies are more likely to want to share reuse libraries with the public. *Government agencies* have played a particularly active role in advancing reuse standards and libraries that are shared with the public.

By law, United States *government procurements* are required to be fair, a virtue valued beyond even effectiveness. In general, government cannot award a follow-on contract to a company simply because it performed well on the predecessor program—a fair competition among interested parties is required and the award will be made based on some combination of proposed actions and estimated cost rather than track record. In this sort of contracting environment, government has an essential need to ensure that one contractor can reuse the products of previous contracts.

The U.S. *Department of Defense* spends 30 billion dollars a year on software. The military may buy software from many suppliers and yet wants what it buys from one supplier to be accessible for reuse by another supplier. The military has developed software reuse guidelines that can be used to standardize contractor performance. One salient such project from the the Department of Defense Advanced Research Projects Agency is called STARS.

One of the key documents from STARS is the *Conceptual Framework for Reuse Processes* (CFRP). CFRP defines a conceptual framework for reuse in terms of the processes involved. The framework is intended to be generic with respect to domains, organizations, economic sectors, methodologies, and technologies. The CFRP identifies the processes involved in reuse and describes at a high level how those processes operate and interact. The management of reuse is described within a spiral of plan, enact, and learn (see Figure 12.2 Reuse Cycle). For instance, in planning one proposes measurements of library assets and their use. These measures then become integral to the evaluation of a reuse project and learning how to change the next plan.

Figure 12.2–Reuse Cycle: This cycle shows the organizational process of reuse that involves planning, enacting, and learning from the experience to plan better for the next enactment.

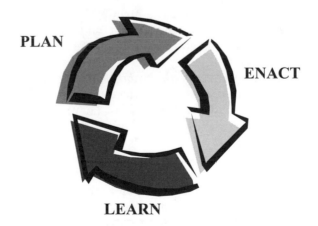

PLAN

ENACT

LEARN

Another STARS document is intended as a planning aid for reuse-based projects. It provides a set of dimensions for characterizing current reuse practice and a suggested process performing the characterization. Both of these STARS documents effectively describe *principles*, but implementation details are left to the organizations which want to adopt STARS. There is a huge gap between the general principles for how an organization might operate so as to achieve software reuse and the specific details of a company's implementation.

Costs and Benefits

Reuse may involve significant change to traditional practice, and there are a number of challenges to overcome in achieving its full benefits. Making software that is reusable generally requires investment above and beyond that required for a one-time system. This effort goes into making the software more flexible, ensuring its quality, and providing additional documentation. Each organization must make decisions about how the investment is supported.

Today's usual contracting methods can create a *disincentive* for contractors to reuse existing software or to provide software for reuse by others. Legal issues arise over liabilities and warranties. Responsibility for maintenance must be identified.

Reuse should reduce maintenance cost. Because proven parts are used, expected defects are fewer. Also, there is a smaller body of software to be maintained. For example, if a maintenance organization is responsible for several different systems with a common graphic user interface, only one fix is required to correct a problem in the user interface rather than one for each system.

Reuse should improve *interoperability* among systems. Through the use of single implementations of interfaces, systems will be able to more effectively interoperate with other systems. For example, if multiple communications systems use a single software package to implement one standard communication protocol, it is very likely that they will be able to interact correctly—more so than when each package is written by a different company but is supposed to follow the same standard.

Another benefit of reuse is support for rapid prototyping. A library of reusable components provides an effective basis for quickly building application prototypes. With these prototypes the software group can get customer feedback on the capability of the system and revise the requirements as dictated by the customer.

With reuse on a small scale—for example, use of a library of mathematical functions—the effort saved from a single reuse is not great; payoff comes from the widespread reuse that is possible. On a *large scale*, entire subsystems, such as an aircraft pilot subsystem, may be reused. However, the opportunities for reuse of a given component are more limited. Large-scale reuse can pay for itself even if a component is only reused once or twice, because of the amount of effort saved.

The effectiveness of reuse will be far greater in some software companies than in others. If a software company or department exclusively develops one kind of application, for example spreadsheets, then it is in the interest of that company to build staff training around a reuse methodology since they will be able to build a library of commonly used spreadsheet components quite quickly. Here it can be expected that projects will be able to make use of large numbers of these components. Companies which have no *specialization* and deal with a large variety of projects with few common elements have less to gain from reuse.

Analogy to Traditional Libraries

Software reuse could not have occurred more than about 50 years ago because there was no software. Document reuse has, however, occurred for centuries, at least. One domain of document reuse is *scientific research*. There reuse by reference is fundamental. A quality research journal article typically contains citations to about 20 other journal articles.

A small *research* team may maintain its own small *library*. Investment in this library may include in the first instance the purchase of subscriptions to some journals. A member of the team may be assigned on a part-time basis to somehow organize the journals in the library so that others can find them.

As research teams cooperate and see the advantage to larger libraries, they may pool their resources. In the extreme case, the national government is convinced to establish a comprehensive library. One example of such a library within the medical domain is the *National Library of Medicine* (NLM) in the U.S.A. NLM subscribes to all 20,000 of the world's biomedical journals. A continual and extensive quality assessment of these journals selects the 3,000 best from the 20,000 and every article within those 3,000 is indexed with about 10 concepts from a thesaurus (Bachrach and Charen, 1978). The thesaurus itself contains about 100,000 concepts and is maintained by a full-time staff of about 10 people. The indexing section of NLM employs about 400 full-time, professional indexers. The results of indexing are distributed world-wide via paper publications, electronic network and CD-ROM. In short, the national level effort to maintain a kind of reuse library is a massive effort. Prior to the summer of 1997, NLM charged users a small fee for hourly connect time to the online database. Since the summer of 1997 access to this online library is completely free to anyone in the wold.

The parallels of the traditional library situation to the software reuse situation are instructive. Software teams that begin a reuse effort will naturally start with a *small library*. Comparable to the journal article citation for software might be a call to a program in the library. As the size of the software library and the number of its users grows, the importance of a systematic approach to the library also increases. National or international efforts may ultimately be the most appropriate.

Researchers who use the NLM system may also write journal articles which would ultimately be indexed in the NLM system. For *publicly-funded*, medical researchers a quantitative measure of success is the number of published, journal articles. For *commercially-funded*, medical researchers the objective may instead be to suggest methods or products which the commercial body can later exploit on the marketplace. Accordingly, the commercially-funded researcher may be forbidden from publishing some research results. For instance, a drug company may not want its researchers to publish work about the new drug which the company is investigating.

Much software is made by companies that do not want to freely contribute their products to a library for other companies to use. The example of *national libraries* of research literature suggests an approach to software reuse. The government could require that successful bidders for a government software development contract would provide the product to a public reuse library. This kind of approach is being taken by the American Department of Defense and may be an important step in the wider acceptance of software reuse methods.

Epilogue

The US Army finished in 1997 an extensive survey of Army personnel responsible for software reuse (Army, 1997b). The survey covered the major areas of Reuse Management, Reuse Education, Domain Analysis, Domain Implementation, and Reusable Asset Acquisition. These are the major areas of interest as regards reuse. The results of the study are consistent with the experiences of other organizations and are the basis for the final *recommendations* of this book.

Many projects reported that they had created a working group to address reuse-related issues and were using reuse language in Requests for Proposals. However, overall adherence to reuse *management* guidelines varied widely from one part of the organization to another part of the organization. The recommendation is for further establishment of connections among projects so that reuse efforts can be further harmonized.

The greatest potential for improvement was documented in the area of *education*. Very few employees have received any significant level of formalized reuse education. However, 70% of staff requested reuse education. Extension of reuse education opportunities should be a high priority.

The results of the *domain analysis* part of the survey was to highlight the importance of high-level domain analysis. This domain analysis should occur not only within an army such as "command and control" but across areas to highlight opportunities for horizontal reuse—namely, reuse across areas. Such further domain analysis would be consistent with the emphasis in software engineering on frameworks or patterns which require high level domain analysis activities. The areas of the organization which show the most overlap in the domain analysis results should be the most appropriate for reuse across areas.

Within *domain implementation*, both opportunistic and systematic reuse activities were reported. To further promote a systematic approach which contributes to greater cost benefits, reuse needs to be incorporated earlier in the software development life cycle. This approach must include varied types of products, such as requirements, designs, architectures, models, application program interfaces, schema, and tests. For each of these different product types, a common set of reuse metrics must be developed, documented, collected, and evaluated.

With regard to *Reusable Asset Acquisition*, an effort needs to be made to extend the availability of reuse repositories and encourage quality donations via an incentive program. This will facilitate an increase in systematic reuse as more products of higher quality and various types are made available. The increasing availability of information across computer networks, particularly the web, leads to the prediction that the contents of reuse repositories will improve in quality and increase in size. However, efforts to reduce the cost of acquisitions implies a reduction in the ability to require reuse features in delivered products. The tension remains between the desire to get a product finished and the desire to contribute a flexible asset to a reuse library.

This book does not per se provide reusable software assets. It does provide a kind of domain analysis of the area of software reuse itself. Furthermore, it serves an education function. The book is available for free across the Internet. The book is also part of an *online course*. The goal of the author is to work with others to build a virtual information technology college for which reuse will be a fundamental tenet.

Contributors to the *Virtual Information Technology College* (Rada, 1997) will include students, teachers, and administrators. Additionally, software developers can contribute to the College by providing software assets that become part of the College. These assets must be provided in such a way that they are open to inspection and fit into the domain model for the College. The infrastructure of the College will be a kind of library of reusable software modules itself.

The *financial incentive* for contributing to the infrastructure will be based on a revenue sharing scheme. The College will be self-financing and each contributed asset that is used will earn a certain percentage of the revenue stream that comes to the College. Of course, this same revenue stream has to pay the human teachers and administrators of the College, but the software is expected to play a very active role in the running of the College and the developers of such software need to be adequately rewarded. Normally an organization has difficulty in adequately defining the financial incentive to software reuse activities but this challenge will be very directly addressed by the Virtual Information Technology College. Other virtual organizations could follow this same model.

Students in the College will be able to examine the infrastructure of their own college to see examples of systematic software reuse. Software reuse will be a key topic in education in this new college. Students that graduate from this College will be better acclimated to a *culture of reuse* and will contribute more effectively to reuse within other organizations.

Appendix I
Selected Glossary

A

application domain: The knowledge and concepts that pertain to a particular computer application area. Examples include battle management, avionics, and nuclear physics. Each application domain can be decomposed into more specialized subdomains where the decomposition is guided by the overall purpose or mission of systems in the domain.

application engineering: The development or evolution of a system to meet particular application requirements.

application generator: A software tool that generates software work products from nonprocedural user specifications of desired capability.

asset: A unit of information of value to a software engineering enterprise. Assets can include a wide variety of items, such as software life cycle products, domain models, processes, documents, and case studies.

asset base: A coherent set of assets, addressing one or more domains and residing in one or more asset libraries.

C

certification: The process of determining to what extent something can be trusted to satisfy its requirements without error.

chief programmer team: A group of people who work together under the guidance of a chief programmer with key support from the team's librarian.

component: Synonymous with asset.

231

constructive cost model: An empirical model of software development effort that is based on several attributes of the anticipated software product, such as its size.

courseware: Software for instructional purposes which often includes multimedia.

D

design: The process of defining the software structure, components, modules, interfaces, and data for an application system to satisfy specified requirements.

document: Any information product, such as a requirements document or a computer program.

document-oriented system: A system in which the integrity of documents is paramount and their available structure in, for instance, Tables of Contents, are needed to provide overviews. In such a system documents are often located by a string search.

domain: An area of activity or knowledge. A number of different classification schemes have been proposed for domains; some of the classes of domains that have been identified include: application, horizontal, and vertical.

domain analysis: The process of identifying, collecting, organizing, analyzing, and modeling domain information by studying and characterizing existing systems, underlying theory, domain expertise, emerging technology, and development histories within a domain of interest. A primary goal is to produce domain models to support the development and evolution of domain assets.

domain engineering: The development and evolution of domain-specific knowledge and assets to support the development and evolution of application systems in a domain. Includes engineering of domain models, architectures, components, generators, methods, and tools.

domain model: A definition of the characteristics of existing and envisioned application products within a domain in terms of what the products have in common and how they may vary.

domain-specific reuse: Reuse in which the reusable assets, the development processes, and the supporting technology are appropriate to, and perhaps developed or tailored for, the application domain for which a system is being developed.

G

generation: A technique or method that involves generating software work product from nonprocedural user specifications of desired capability.

H

horizontal domain: The knowledge and concepts that pertain to particular functional capabilities that can be utilized across more than one application domain. Examples include user interfaces, database systems, and statistics. Most horizontal domains can be decomposed into more specialized subdomains where the decomposition is often guided by characteristics of the solution software.

I

interpretive indexing: The assignment of concepts to a document to indicate its fundamental meaning.

L

legacy systems: Software systems in domains of interest that can impart legacy knowledge about the domains and feed domain analysis or reengineering efforts to produce domain assets or new application systems.

library: A collection of components, together with the procedures and support functions required to provide the components to users.

library data model: The information (sometimes called meta-data) that describes the structure of the data in an asset library.

life cycle: The stages a software or software-related product passes through from its inception until it is no longer useful.

life cycle model: A model describing the processes, activities, and tasks involved in the development and maintenance of software and software related products, spanning the products' life cycles.

M

methodology: A set or system of methods and principles for achieving a goal such as producing a software system.

'Not Invented Here' Syndrome: The situation when developers are unwilling to reuse software that was developed elsewhere because it was 'not invented here'. Software engineers enjoy the creative aspects of their profession, and can feel that these are diminished when reusing someone else's software.

O

object-oriented system: A system in which objects and their relations are paramount. Hierarchical relations are particularly important as they support inferencing along inheritance paths.

opportunistic reuse: The ad hoc reuse of assets in the development of software systems using a software development process that has not been altered to accommodate systematic reuse. In opportunistic reuse, the developer determines where reuse can be applied to develop a software system without the organized use of domain engineering products during successive stages of a software engineering process.

organizing: The collecting, analyzing, indexing and storing of information so that it can be easily accessed later.

P

portability: The extent to which a software component originally developed on one computer and operating system can be used on another computer and operating system.

precision: A measure of the ability to reject non-relevant materials.

process: A description of a series of steps, actions, or activities to bring about a desired result.

process-driven software engineering: An approach in which software is developed or evolved in accordance with well defined, repeatable processes that are subject to continuous measurement and improvement and are enforced through management policies.

Q

query: A request for identification of a set of assets, expressed in terms of a set of criteria which the identified items must satisfy.

R

recall: measures the ability of a system to retrieve relevant documents.

reorganizing: The tailoring of information to suit a new purpose after that information has been first organized into a library and then retrieved from that library.

requirement: A condition or capability that must be met or possessed by a software system or software-related product.

retrieval system: an automated tool that supports classification and retrieval of assets.

reusability: the extent to which information is able to be reused.

reuse: The application of existing information. In software engineering, reuse usually involves the application of information encoded in software-related work products. A simple example of the reuse of software work products is reuse of subroutine libraries for string manipulations or mathematical calculations. A simple example of the reuse of information not encoded in software work products is consultation with a human expert to obtain desired knowledge.

reuse-based software engineering: An approach to software-intensive system development in which systems are constructed principally from existing software assets rather than through new development.

reuse cycle: One pass through the Reuse Planning, Enactment, and Learning processes in a particular reuse program.

reuse infrastructure: The collection of capabilities that is needed to support and sustain reuse projects within a reuse program. Includes tools and technology; organizational structure, policies, and procedures; and education and training.

reuse library: A set of assets and associated services for accessing and reusing the assets. A library typically consists of assets, corresponding asset descriptions, a library data model, and a set of services (manual or automated) for managing, finding, retrieving, and reusing assets. Such services can include reuse consultation services.

reuse library interoperability: The ability of two or more distinct, heterogeneous Software reuse Libraries to dynamically provide access to the other's Assets, Asset descriptions, and other available information.
reuser: An individual or organization that reuses assets. reverse engineering: The process of analyzing a computer system's software to identify components and their interrelationships.

S

software engineering environment: The computer hardware, operating system, tools, and encoded processes and rules that an individual software engineer works with to develop a software system.

specification: A document or formal representation that prescribes, in a precise manner, the requirements, design, behavior, or other characteristics of a software product.

T

tailoring: The process of adapting products for application in new, specific situations.

thesaurus: A set of concepts in which each concept may have hierarchical and associative relations to other concepts. A concept is labeled with a preferred term. Synonymous or non-preferred terms are also provided.

traceability: The characteristic of software-related products that documents the derivation path.

W

word frequency indexing: An automatic assignment of words to a document based on their frequency of occurrence in the documents.

Appendix II
References

William Agresti, "Framework for a Flexible Development Process," *New Paradigms for Software Development*, edited by William Agresti, pp. 11-14, IEEE, New York, 1986.

Hanne Albrechtsen, "Software Concepts: Knowledge Organisation and the Human Interface," *Tools for Knowledge Organisation and the Human Interface*, pp. 48-63, INDEKS Verlag, Frankfurt, Germany, 1990.

Army Reuse Center "Library Tool Demonstration" http://arc_www.belvoir.army.mil/demos2.htm, 1997.

Army Reuse Center, *Reuse Technology Assessment Report for the Department of the Army*, HQ USAISSC, Fort Belvoir, VA, April 30, and also at http://arc_www.belvoir.army.mil/, 1997b.

A. Avner, "Production of computer-based instructional materials," *Issues in Instructional Systems Development*, Edited by H.F. O'Neil, Jr, pp. 133-180, Academic Press, New York, 1979.

AICC (1995) "Courseware Interchange Guidelines and Recommendations" from *Aviation Industry CBT Committee Courseware Interchange, AGR 007, Version 1.0* by Courseware Technology Subcommittee at http://www.aicc.org/ agr007.htm

AICC (1997) "Computer Managed Instruction Guidelines and Recommendations" from *Aviation Industry CBT Committee Computer Managed Instruction, AGR 006, Version 1.1* by CMI Subcommittee at http://www.aicc.org/agr006.htm

C. Bachrach, T. Charen, "Selection of MEDLINE Contents, the Development of its Thesaurus, and theIndexing Process," *Medical Informatics, Vol. 3, N 3*, pp. 237-254, 1978.

T. F. Baker, "Chief Programmer Team management of production programming," *IBM Systems Journal*, Vol. 11, N 1, 1972.

James Baldo, Jr., James Moore, David Rine "Software Reuse Standards" *StandardView*, 5, 2, pp. 50-57, June 1997.

R. Balzer "Transformational Implementation: An Example," *IEEE Transactions on Software Engineering*, Vol. 7, pp. 3-14, January 1981.

Paul G. Bassett Framing *Software Reuse: Lessons from the Real World* Yourdon Press: New Jersey, 1997.

Don Batory, Vivek Singhal, Marty Sirkin, Jeff Thomas, "Scalable Software Libraries," *ACM SIGSOFT '93*, Vol. 18, N 5, pp. 191-199, December 1993.

D. Bauer, "A Reusable Parts Center," *IBM Systems Journal*, 32, 4, pp. 620-624, 1993.

T. E. Bell, D C Bixler, M E Dyer, "An Extendable Approach to Computer Aided Software Requirements Engineering," *IEEE Transactions Software Engineering*, Vol. 3, N 1, pp. 49-60, 1977.

Bell Canada *Trillium - Telecom Product Development Process Capability Model*, Bell Northern Research, Nortel, 1994.

James Bigelow, "Hypertext and CASE," *IEEE Computer*, pp. 23-27, March 1988.

T.J. Biggerstaff, "Design Recovery for Maintenance and Reuse," *Computer*, pp. 36-49, July 1989.

B. W. Boehm, "Software Engineering Economics," Prentice-Hall, Englewood Cliffs, New Jersey, 1981.

Boeing Company, IBM Federal Systems Company, Unisys Corporation, *STARS Conceptual Framework for Reuse Processes (CFRP), Volume 1: Definition, Version 3.0*, United States Air Force, Hanscom Air Force Base, Massachusettes, October 25, 1993.

Boeing Company *Reuse Strategy Model: Planning Aid for Reuse-based Projects*, CDRL 5159, Task U03, STARS Program, Contract #F19628-88-D-0028, July 31, 1993

Grady Booch *Object-Oriented Analysis and Design with Applications, 2nd edition*, Redwood City, CA: Benjamin Cummings, 1994.

James M. Boyle, Monagur N. Muralidharan, "Program Reusability through Program Transformation," *IEEE Transactions on Software Engineering*, Vol. 10(5), pp. 574-588, September 1984.

F. Brooks, *The Mythical Man-Month*, Addison-Wesley, 1975.

Davide Brugali, Giuseepe Menga, Amund Aarsten "The Framework Life Span" *Communications of the ACM*, 40, 10, pp 65-68, 1997

Bruce A. Burton, Rhonda Wienk Aragon, Stephen A. Bailey, Kenneth D. Koehler, Lauren A. Mayes, "The Reusable Software Library," *IEEE Software*, 4, pp. 25-33, July 1987.

Gianluigi Caldiera, Victor R. Basili, "Identifying and Qualifying Reusable Software Components," Vol. 24, N 2, pp. 61-70, *IEEE Software*, 1991.

Brad Campbell, Joseph M. Goodman, "HAM: A General Purpose Hypertext Abstract Machine," *Communications of the ACM*, Vol. 31, N 7, pp. 856-861, July 1988.

Lionel Cartwright, "AISE Software Portability Project - Review of Step 2," *AISE Year Book*, pp. 94-97, 1985.

J. M. Caruso, D R Hancock, "The business case for reuse," *IBM Systems Journal*, Vol. 32, N 4, pp. 567-594, 1993.

Chaomei Chen, Roy Rada, "A Conceptual Model for Supporting Collaborative Authoring and Reuse," *Knowledge Organization*, Vol. 21, N 2, pp. 88-93, 1994.

Alistair Cockburn, "The Interaction of Social Issues and Software Architecture," *Communications of the ACM*, 59, 10, pp 40-46, 1996.

National Library and Information Associations Council, *Guidelines for Thesaurus Structure, Construction and Use*, American National Standards Institute, New York, 1980.

N. Delisle, M. Schwartz, "Neptune: A Hypertext System for CAD Applications," *Proceedings of ACM SIGMOD International Conference on Management of Data*, pp. 132-143, 1986.

DoD (Department of Defense) Software Reuse Initiative, *DoD Software Reuse Vision and Strategy. Technical Report 1222-04-210/40*, Center for Software Reuse Operations, Alexandria, Virginia, 1992.

DoD (Department of Defense) Software Reuse Initiative, *DoD Software Executive Primer*, Center for Software Reuse Operations, Alexandria, Virginia, 1995.

DoD (Department of Defense) Software Reuse Initiative, *Software Reuse Business Model Technical Report*, Center for Software Reuse Operations, Alexandria, Virginia, 1995.

F. DeRemer, H Kron, "Programming-in-the-large versus programming-in-the-small," *IEEE Transactions on Software Engineering*, Vol. 2, pp. 80-86, 1976.

Chris Edwards, Nigel Savage, Ian Walden, *Information Technology and the Law*, MacMillan Publishers Ltd., London, 1990.

EOE "What is the Educational Object Economy" *Educational Object Economies*, http://trp.research.apple.com, 1997.

Educom "IMS Metadata Executive Summary" *IMS Metadata*, http://www.imsproject.org/ metadata/MDexec.html, 1997.

Mohamed Fayad and Douglas C Schmidt "Object-Oriented Application Frameworks" *Communications of the ACM*, 40, 10, pp 32-38, 1997

Martin Fowler, *Analysis Patterns: reusable object models*, Addison Wesley: Massachusetts, 1997

W.B. Frakes, P.B. Gandel, "Representing Reusable Software," *Information Software Technology*, Vol. 32, N 10, pp. 653-664, December, 1990.

D. Garlan, R Allen, J Ockerbloom "Architectural Mismatch: Why reuse is so hard" *IEEE Software*, November, 1995

Adele Goldberg, Steve Abell, David Leibs "The LearningWorks Development and Delivery Frameworks" *Communications of the ACM*, 40, 10, pp 78-81, 1997

R Goldman-Segall, "Interpreting Video Data: Introducing a 'Significance Measure' to Layer Descriptions," J*ournal of Educational Multimedia and Hypermedia*, Vol. 2, N 3, pp. 261-281, 1993.

Michael Gordon, Manfred Kochen, "Recall-Precision Trade-Off: A Derivation," *Journal of the American Society for Information Science*, Vol. 40, N 3, pp. 145-151, 1989.

C. Green, S. Westfold, "Knowledge-Based Programming Self-Applied," *Machine Intelligence*, Vol. 10, New York, Wiley, 1982.

M. L. Griss, "Software Reuse: from library to factory," *IBM Systems Journal*, 32, 4, pp. 548-566, 1993.

Ralph E Johnson "Frameworks=(Components+Patterns)" *Communications of the ACM*, 40, 10, pp 39-42, 1997

M. Halstead, "Elements of Software Science," Elsevier, New York, 1977.

Jean Hartmann, David J. Robson, "Techniques for Selective Revalidation," *IEEE Software*, pp. 31-36, 1990.

Philip A. Hausler, Mark G. Pleszkoch, Richard C. Linger, R. Hevner, "Using Function Abstraction to Understand Program Behavior," *IEEE Software*, pp. 55-63, January 1990.

K Hayashi and A Sekijima, "Mediating interface between hypertext and structured documents," *Electronic Publishing: origination, dissemination and design*, Vol. 6, N 4, pp. 423-434, 1993.

J. Heidepriem, "Trends in Process Control of Metal Rolling," *Proceedings of the 11th IFAC World Congress*, Vol. 11, pp. 138-147, Tallinn/Estland, 1990a.

Robert R. Holibaugh, Sholom G. Cohen, Kyo C. Kang, Spencer Peterson, "Reuse where to begin and why," *Proceedings of Tri-Ada'89*, pp. 266-277, ACM Press, New York, 1989.

IEEE Standards Committee, "IEEE Standard for Software Quality Assurance Plans," *IEEE*, New York, 1981.

IEEE Software Engineering Standards Committee, *Strategy Statement*, August 20, 1995.

IMSL "Library User's Manual 1.0 Edition,," Houston, Texas, 1987.

ISO "Documentation - Command for interactive text searching (ISO/DIS 8777)," 1986.

T. Capers Jones, "Measuring Programming Quality and Productivity," *IBM Systems Journal*, Vol. 17, N 1, pp. 39-63, 1978.

T. Capers Jones, "Reusability in Programming: A Survey of the State of the Art," *IEEE Transactions on Software Engineering*, Vol. 10, N 5, pp. 488-494, September 1984.

Rebecca Joos, "Software Reuse at Motorola," *IEEE Software*, Vol. 11, N 5, pp. 42-47, September, 1994.

Gail E. Kaiser, David Garlan, "Melding Software Systems from Reusable Building Blocks," *IEEE Software*, pp. 17-24, July 1987.

Simon Kaplan, Yoelle Maarek, "Incremental Maintenance of Semantic Links in Dynamically Changing Hypertext," *Interacting with Computers*, Vol. 2, N 3, pp. 337-366, 1990.

Susan Katz, "Glossary of Software Reuse Terms," *NIST Special Publication 500-222*, National Institute of Standards and Technology (NIST),1994.

B. W. Kernighan, R Pike, "The Unix Programming Environment," Prentice-Hall, Englewood Cliffs, New Jersey, 1984.

George L. Kovacs, "Software Reuse and Standardization for SMEs—the CIM-EXP Perspective" StandardView, 5, 2, pp. 58-60, 1997.

C.W. Kreuger, "Software reuse," *ACM Computing Surveys*, Vol. 24, N 2, pp. 131-183, 1992.

Krishnamurthy, Balachander. *Practical Reusable Unix Software*. John Wiley & Sons, 1995.

J. Lahore, G. Dworkin, "Information Technology: The Challenge to Copyright," Sweet and Maxwell, London, U.K., 1984.

Manfred Lenz, Hans Albrecht Schmid, Peter Wolf, "Software Reuse Through Building Blocks," *IEEE Software*, pp. 34-42, July 1987.

Lim, Wayne C, *Managing Software Reuse*. Prentice Hall, 1995.

C. Lung, J.E. Urban, "Integration of domain analysis and analogical approach for software reuse," *Proceedings of the 1993 ACM/SIGAPP Symposium on Applied Computing*, Edited by E Deaton, K.M. George, H Bergel, G Hedrick, pp. 48-53, ACM Press, New York, 1993.

Stan Magee and Leonard Tripp, *Software Engineering Standards and Specifications: An Annotated Index and Directory*, Global Professional Publications, Denver, 1994.

U. Margiotta, R. Picco, "An item banking service: pre-project for a national system of evaluation," tools, *Proceedings of the NATO Research Workshop*, Editted by D.A. Leclercq, J.E. Bruno, pp. 12-18, Springer-Verlag, Berlin, Germany, 1993.

I.M. Marshall, W.B. Samson, P.I. Dugard, "Multimedia courseware cost modelling," *European Cost Modelling Conference '94*, pp. 27.1-27.18, 1994.

Yoshihiro Matsumoto, "A Software Factory: An Overall Approach to Software Production," *Tutorial: Software Reusability*, pp. 155-178, IEEE Computer Society Press, 1987.

G. M. McCue, "IBM's Santa Teresa Laboratory - Architectural Design for Program," Development, *IBM Systems Journal*, Vol. 17, pp. 4-25, 1978.

Bertran Meyer, *Object-Oriented Software Construction*, Prentice Hall International, Hempstead, England, 1988.

Hafedh Mili, "SoftClass: An Object-Oriented Tool for Software Reuse," *Proceedings of TOOLS USA '91*, Santa Barbara, California, 1991.

Hafedh Mili, Roy Rada, Weigang Wang, Karl Strickland, Cornelia Boldyreff, Lene Olsen, Jan Witt, Jurgen Heger, Wolfgang Scherr, Peter Elzer, "Practitioner and SoftClass: A Comparative Study of Two Software Reuse Research Projects," *Journal of Systems and Software*, Vol. 25, N 2, pp. 147-171, 1994.

Hafedh Mili, Fatma Mili, Ali Mili, "Software Reuse: Issues and Research Directions," *IEEE Transactions on Software Engineering*, Vol. 21, No. 6, June 1996 .

Hafedh Mili, Roy Rada, "Merging Thesauri: Principles and Evaluation,"*IEEE Transactions on Pattern Analysis and Machine Intelligence*, Vol. 10,N 2, pp. 204-220, 1988.

Harlan D. Mills, Richard C. Linger, Alan R. Hevner, *Principles of Information System Analysis and Design*, Academic Press, 1986.

James Moore and Roy Rada "Organizational Badge Collecting" *Communications of the ACM*, 39, 8 pp 17-21, August 1996.

National Bureau of Standards (NBS), *Guidelines for Documentation of Computer Programs and Automated Systems*, FIPS Publication 38, 1976.

J. M. Neighbors, "DRACO: A Method for Engineering Reusable Software Systems," *Software Reusability, Concepts and Models*, Vol. 1, pp. 295-320, ACM Press, New York, 1989 (from the 1984 article in *IEEE Transactions on Software Engineering*, Vol. 10).

Jakob Nielson, *Coordinating User Interfaces for Consistency*, Academic Press, 1989.

S.H. Oh, Y.J. Lee, M.H Kim, "Knowledge-based software components for qualitative measurement of DBMS," *Proceedings the 2nd international conference on Expert Systems for Development*, pp. 69-73, IEEE Computer Society Press, Los Alamitos, California, 1994.

Paramax Systems Corporation, *Direction-Level Handbook: Central Archive for Reusable Defense Software (CARDS)*, STARS-AC-04104/001/00, September 24, 1992.

D. Parnas, "The Role of Program Specification," *Research Directions in Software Technology*, Edited by P. Wegner, MIT Press, Cambridge, Massachusetts, 1979.

A Pentland, R Picard, G Davenport, R Welsh, "The BT/MIT Project on Advanced Image Tools for Telecommunications: an Overview," *Proceedings 2nd International Conference on Image Communications*, 1993.

D. Persico, L. Sarti, Viarengo, "Browsing a Database of Multimedia Learning Material," *Interactive Learning International*, Vol. 8, pp. 213-235, 1992.

Jeffrey Poulin, *Measuring Software Reuse: principles practices and economic models*, Addison Wesley, 1997

Ruben Prieto-Diaz, Peter Freeman, "Classifying Software for Reusability," *IEEE Software*, pp. 6-16, January 1987.

Defense Information Systems Agency (DISA), *Domain Analysis and Design Process, Version 1 Technical Report, 1222-04-210/301.1*, Center for Information Management, Software Reuse Program, Arlington, Virginaia, March, 1993.

Roy Rada, *Hypertext: from Text to Expertext*, McGraw-Hill, London, 1991.

Roy Rada, "Hypertext writing and document reuse: the role of a semantic net," *Electronic Publishing*, Vol. 3, N 3, pp. 3-13, 1990.

Roy Rada, George S Carson, Chris Haynes "Standards: the Role of Consensus " *Communications of the ACM*, 37, 3 pp 15-16, April 1994

Roy Rada, Weigang Wang, Hafedh Mili, Jurgen Heger, Wolfgang Scherr, "Software Reuse: from Text to Hypertext," *Software Engineering Journal*, pp. 311-321, September 1992.

Roy Rada, *Interactive Media*, Springer-Verlag, New York, 1995.

Roy Rada, Geeng-Neng You, "Balanced Outlines and Hypertext," *Journal of Documentation*, Vol. 48, N 1, pp. 20-44, March 1992.

Roy Rada, Barbara Keith, Marc Burgoine, Steven George, David Reid, "Collaborative Writing of Text and Hypertext," *Hypermedia*, Vol. 1, N 2, pp. 93-110, 1989.

Roy Rada, Joyce Backus, Tom Giampa, Subash Goel, Christina Gibbs, "Computerized Guides to Journal Selection," *Information Technology and Libraries*, Vol. 6, N 3, pp. 173-184, 1987.

Roy Rada and John Berg "Standards: Free or Sold?" *Communications of the ACM*, 38, 2 pp 23-27, February 1995

Roy Rada "Systems for Reusing Hypermedia Courseware," *Multimedia Tools and Applications*, 2 pp 53-78, 1996.

Roy Rada *Virtual Education Manifesto* http://www.gnacademy.org/, Hypermedia Solutions Limited, 1997

S. R. Ranganathan, *Prolegomena to Library Classification*, 3rd Edition., Asion Publishing House: Bombay, India, 1937.

Charles Rich, Richard Waters, "Automatic Programming: Myths and Prospects," *IEEE Computer*, pp. 40-51, August 1988.

SAIS/ASSET "Asset Source for Software Engineering Technology" *http://www.asset.com/*, 1997.

Douglas Schmidt, Mohamed Fayad, Ralph Johnson "Introduction to Software Patterns" *Communications of the ACM*, 39, 10, pp. 36-39, 1996.

Software Technology for Adaptable Reliable Systems (STARS), *The Reuse-Oriented Software Evolution (ROSE) Process Model, Version 0.5*, Unisys STARS Technical Report STARS-UC-05155/001/00, Advanced Research Projects Agency, STARS Technology Center, Arlington, Virginia, July, 1993.

Software Technology for Adaptable Reliable Systems (STARS), *Organisation Domain Modelling (ODM), Volume I - Conceptual Foundations, Process and Workproduct Descriptions, Version 0.5 - DRAFT*, Unisys STARS, Advanced Research Projects Agency, STARS Technology Center, Arlington, Virginia, July, 1993b.

Spencer Ruigaber, Stephen B. Ornburn, Richard J. LeBlanc Jr., "Recognising Design Decisions in Programs," *IEEE Software*, pp. 46-54, January 1990.

Gerard Salton, Michael McGill, "Introduction to Modern Information Retrieval," McGraw-Hill, New York, 1983.

C. Saurel, "An Expert System Aiding Development Engineering Software Packages," *Expert System and their Applications, Avignon*, France, 1985.

SESC Software Engineering Standards Committee, *Master Plan for Software Engineering Standards, Version 1.0*, IEEE Standards Committee, December 1, 1993,

P M. Senge, *The Fifth Discipline*, Doubleday/Currency, New York, 1990.

Geoffrey Leslie Simons, "What is Software Engineering?," NCC Publications, Manchester, England, 1987.

D. Smith, G Kotik, S Westfold, "Research on knowledge-based software environments at Kestrel Institute," *IEEE Transactions on Software Engineering*, Vol. 11, pp. 1278-1295, November 1985.

Software Productivity Consortium *Domain Engineering Guidebook, Version 01.00.03*, SPC-92019-CMC, December 1992.

Ian Sommerville, *Software Engineering*, 5th Edition, Addison-Wesley, Reading, Massachusetts, 1996.

Giancarlo Succi, Luigi Benedicenti, Paolo Predonzani, Tullio Vernazza "Standardizing the Reuse of Software Processes" *StandardView*, 5, 2, pp. 74-83, 1997

GTE Government Systems, NATO *Standard for Management of a Reusable Software Component Library*, NATO Communications and Information Systems Agency, Brussels, Belgium, March 1992a.

GTE Government Systems, NATO *Standard for Software Reuse Procedures*, NATO Communications and Information Systems Agency, Brussels, Belgium, March 1992b.

GTE Government Systems, *NATO Standard for Development of Reusable Software Components*, NATO Communications and Information Systems Agency, Brussels, Belgium, March 1992c.

J. R. Tiro, H Gregorius, "Management of Reuse at IBM," *IBM Systems Journal*, Vol. 32, N 4, pp. 612-615, 1993.

W. Tracz, "Software Reuse Myths," *ACM SIGSOFT Software Engineering Notes*, Vol. 13, N 1, pp. 17-21, 1988.

Will Tracz *Confessions of a Used Program Salesman: Institutionalizing Software Reuse*. Addison-Wesley, 1995.

Virginia Center of Excellence for Software Reuse and Technology Transfer, *Reuse Adoption Guidebook. Technical Report SPC-92051-CMC*, Software Productivity Consortium, Herndon, Virginia, November, 1992.

USAF (United States Armed Forces) *Guidelines for Successful Acquisition and Management of Software Intensive Systems: Weapons Systems, Command and Control Systems, Management Information Systems*, Department of the Air Force, Software Technology Support Center, February 1995.

USAF (United States Armed Forces) *Software Reuse Guidelines, ASQB-GI-90-015*, U.S. Army Institute for Research in Management Information, Communications and Computer Sciences, April 1990.

M. Wasmund, "Implementing Critical Success Factors in Software Reuse," *IBM Systems Journal*, Vol. 32, N 4, pp. 595-611, 1993.

G. M. Weinberg, *The Psychology of Computer Programming*, Van Nostrand, New York, 1971.

Edmond Weiss, "USABILITY: Stereotypes and Traps," *Text, ConText, and HyperText*, Edited by E Barrett, pp. 175-185, MIT Press: Cambridge, Massachusetts, 1988.

Scott N. Woodfield, David W Embley, Del T Scott, "Can Programmers Reuse Software?," *IEEE Software*, pp. 52-59, July 1987.

Surya B. Yadav, Ralph R. Bravoco, Akemi T Chatfield, T M Rjkumar, "Comparison of Analysis Techniques for Information Requirements Determination," *Communications of the ACM*, Vol. 31, N 9, pp. 1090-1097, 1988.

United States Navy (USN), *Weapon System Software Development*, *MIL-STD-1679*, 1976.

Wieringa, R.B. and R.J. Feenstra. *Information Systems: Correctness and Reusability*—Selected Papers from the IS-CORE Workshop, Amsterdam, September 1994. World Scientific, 1995.

P. J. Williams, P Hammond, "The Creation of Electronic Visual Archives for Teaching and Learning," *Proceedings of the 12th UK Eurographics Conference*, 1994.

William Wong "A Management Overview of Software Reuse," *NIST Special Publication 500-142*, National Institute of Standards and Technology (NIST),1986.

William Wong "Management Guide to Software Reuse," *NIST Special Publication 500-155*, National Institute of Standards and Technology (NIST),1988

R. T. Yeh, P Zave, "Specifying Software Requirements," *Proceedings IEEE*, Vol. 68, N 9, pp. 1077-85, Institute of Electrical and Electronics Engineers, New York, 1980.

Clement T. Yu, Gerard Salton, "Effective Information Retrieval Using Term Accuracy" *Communications of the ACM*, 20, 3, pp 135-142, 1997.

A. Zanger (editor) *Andrew View Newsletter, Volume 5, Number 2*, ftp://ftp.andrew.cmu.edu/pub/AUIS/NEWSLETTERS/ASCII/96 Summer.ascii, 1996

Index

249